Critical Times for America

Westar Studies

The **Westar Studies** series offers distinctive scholarly publications on topics related to the field of Religious Studies. The studies seek to be multi-dimensional both in terms of the subject matter addressed and the perspective of the author. Westar Studies are not related to Westar seminars but offer scholars a deliberate space of free inquiry to engage both scholarly peers and the public.

Critical Times for America

The Politics of Cultural Amnesia

Burton L. Mack

CASCADE *Books* • Eugene, Oregon

CRITICAL TIMES FOR AMERICA
The Politics of Cultural Amnesia

Westar Studies

Copyright © 2019 Burton L. Mack. All rights reserved. Except for brief quotations in critical publications or reviews, no part of this book may be reproduced in any manner without prior written permission from the publisher. Write: Permissions, Wipf and Stock Publishers, 199 W. 8th Ave., Suite 3, Eugene, OR 97401.

Cascade Books
An Imprint of Wipf and Stock Publishers
199 W. 8th Ave., Suite 3
Eugene, OR 97401

www.wipfandstock.com

PAPERBACK ISBN: 978-1-5326-7952-0
HARDCOVER ISBN: 978-1-5326-7953-7
EBOOK ISBN: 978-1-5326-7954-4

Cataloguing-in-Publication data:

Names: Mack, Burton L., author.

Title: Critical times for America : the politics of cultural amnesia / Burton L. Mack.

Description: Eugene, OR: Cascade Books, 2019. | Westar Studies. | Includes bibliographical references.

Identifiers: ISBN 978-1-5326-7952-0 (paperback) | ISBN 978-1-5326-7953-7 (hardcover) | ISBN 978-1-5326-7954-4 (ebook)

Subjects: LCSH: Memory—Social aspects. | Regionalism—North America—History. | Civilization, Western.

Classification: BL60 M2761 2019 (print). | BL60 (ebook).

Scripture quotations are taken from the New Revised Standard Version Bible, copyright © 1989 National Council of the Churches of Christ in the United States of America. Used by permission. All rights reserved worldwide.

Manufactured in the U.S.A.   09/20/19

Contents

Introduction: The Big Picture | 1

1. Monarchy and Madness: The Quest for a Principle of Authority | 9
2. Nations and Races: America's History of Eleven Nations | 26
3. Cultural Amnesia: Intellectual Voices in the Wilderness | 50
4. Social Anthropology: The Causes of Human Aggression | 67
5. Social Democracy: Intelligence or Despair | 87

Conclusion: Repainting the Big Picture | 105
Bibliography | 109

Introduction
The Big Picture

My study of the *social issues* that were confronting America at the end of the long and lively history of Western Civilization had just gone to press at Yale University when a new president of the United States was elected, a president who had no interest in these social issues, much less the health and well-being of the Nation as a whole. Just when the mood of the people was ready, I thought, to resist the myopic Tea Party Republicans and build on the Democratic legacy of enlightened policies and platforms, a wealthy tycoon appeared, strutting in front of the cameras, posing as a monarch, and threatening the very best of our Democratic achievements since FDR. These achievements were hard won legislations for civil rights, carefully crafted attempts to control the economy in the interest of fairness and well-being, a comprehensive medical insurance for all the people, putting into place governmental agencies to administer legal and social welfare, a foreign policy that called for negotiation instead of threats, conflict, and war, treaties to reduce nuclear weapons and the threat of war, and a global plan to address the problem of climate change caused by industrial society. Trump targeted every one of these achievements for repeal in the interest of American business. Oh my, I said to myself, the promise of America at the end of the Western tradition is not working. Capitalism has become a self-conscious political power and is now in the hands of a wealthy business man with an adolescent mentality. He is in the process of threatening the well-being of our society by subverting our democracy from the top down in Washington and disbanding our democratic institutions and policies throughout the land. I was stunned. I had been thinking that the social issues that had developed during the last century could actually be solved if we kept working on what I understood to be America's pursuit of a modern multicultural and common good democracy. Now it seemed that although those issues were still there, they had been looked upon as the creation of a wrong headed Democratic party in power, set aside by a single issue Republican mentality, and disregarded by an egotistical president whose concept of "greatness" for America was dismantling both our promise and our place in the modern world. How could that be?

As a biblical scholar and historian of religion I knew something about religion, human values, and social formations. I had been working on the origins of the Christian myth during the Greco-Roman period and on the influence of the myth (as encoded in the Bible and especially in the gospels) in the formation of Catholic Christianity (as Christendom). My questions about the Christian myth had always been about the effective difference it made for the way in which a society understood itself and functioned. In the case of Christendom (during the Roman Empire) the relation of the myth to the worldview and practices of the Catholic Church and its empires was more or less obvious. But as the Reformation came into view in the course of my review of the history of Western civilization, the big picture of Christendom became fragmented and took the shape of the many smaller kingdoms of modernity (as Nation States). Thus the social effectiveness of the Christian myth that belonged to the big picture of Christendom was also fragmented, and different readings of both the myth and of its picture of history and cosmos were being parceled out to the various European nations as separate and somewhat distinct (petty) kingdoms. The fundamental logic of the myth about the importance of morals and piety for religious persons did remain as the ethic for individual Christians and as an ethos for Protestant congregations and churches, but its social logic that divided the world between Christians and pagans could no longer be working. The Christian anthropology was a division of Christians and pagans that could no longer be used to describe the place of Christianity in the European world or the place of Christian America in the worlds of the many peoples and cultures that were coming into view. Neither could it still support the Church's sense of mission to the world in the interest of a universal Christianity. Christian mentality could still work to support personal religious

Introduction

experience and justify a particular Christian community or denomination, but the social logic of the myth as the singular rationale for a unified and common Christian culture was no longer possible in a time of many cultures and nations. Individual scenarios from the Bible and its narrative logic (myth) could still be at work as subtle markers and taboos in different churches, and thus be cultivated as the basis for their beliefs and practices, but viewed together these fragmented features of an erstwhile biblical ethos lost the coherence they had when linked to the central events and agencies of the big picture of Catholic Christianity. The world became an arena for many streams of collective interests that emerged in the Rennaisance and Enlightenment that were not generated by Christianity. And the Christian churches since the Reformation formed separate sects and institutions. This means that the modern period of Western history has raised the question of the effective difference Christianity has made and may still be making in the human enterprise of social formation. In the field of religious studies this question is made more precise by asking about the social logic of the Christian myth. In order to do that it is necessary to have a social theory of myth (religion) and some way of accounting for a people's collective mythic mentality and way of thinking.

Starting with tribal societies in conversation with ethnographers, I tackled the problem by noting the close relation between a tribes's religion (myths and rituals) and their fundamental practices. I used the term *social interests* to refer to the ideas, activities, and practices common to a particular society as a collection of individuals who accepted and understood their own patterns of activity and practices as the way their tribe worked for the benefit of all. The social interests pertaining to the origins of Christianity were all matters of finding a place for a new cross-cultural social identity in the Greco-Roman world of cultural disruptions. The social interests were largely matters of group formations, intellectual activities, and leadership justifications for multiethnic groups and schools seeking a (mythic) rationale for their links to Hebrew and Greek histories and cultures in the midst of the Hellenistic period of Western civilization. I have told this story rather more fully in earlier publications. The social interests that evolved in the later history of the Western tradition, however, were all matters of another sort. They were truly amazing intellectual discoveries, inventions, and achievements of human beings who had begun to explore the larger natural world in which they lived, human accomplishments not related directly to the problems of cultural legacy, and not generated by the Christian myth at all. They included the Rennaissance awareness of the individual and its place in the natural world, Science and its pursuits of worldly knowledge and technology; the Enlightenment and its self-consciousness about the functional importance of language, memory, and history for human experience and culture; Industry and its ability to create machines and material culture; Capitalism and its ability to create financial systems and global markets; Colonialism and its effects on empires, global markets, and wealth as the new register of personal and institutional power and influence. None of these interests can be blamed individually for the social issues that have arisen in the course of their cultivation and development as streams of particular interests that now energize and drive our social formations. But each is clearly involved in the dynamics of the modern world that has become problematic at the seams where two or more social interests intersect or overlap. The primary problem is that all of these interests have developed distinct institutions and bodies of self-understanding (including mythologies) that support their projects. None of these interests has the human social enterprise in view as a comprehensive working system in the interest of the common good and well-being of the society as a whole. The investments of energy in them, and their organization for short term practical results are driven by their own self-interests. None of them as separate configurations of energy and purpose has any way of braking its speed of production. None has any internal reason to consider the consequences of its pursuits for other features of the society and world at large. Some of the social issues that have resulted from this blindness and self-centeredness include: (1) global warming and the threat of ecological disaster related to single-minded industrial pursuits; (2) exploitations of other peoples and their natural resources in the interest of our own industries; (3) arms proliferation for national defense, and gun violence for profit; (4) the huge gaps between the wealthy and the poor that occur in economies without governmental regulation; (5) the formation of private militias for ideological reasons in America and for political reasons in countries we have influenced abroad; (6) military incursions into other nations to protect corporate interests; (7) ethnic cleansings and massacres around the world (not all of which have been directly instigated by America); and (8) the threat of nuclear war related to conflicts for power. However, as serious as the social situation has become, it was still possible, I thought, to imagine solutions for these issues. I was working with a "big picture" theory of religion and culture that was essentially constructive with an anthropology that did not

Introduction

need conquest, war, and violence. And, given the obvious features of self-interest at work within the social interests as pursuits, the concerns of the Amercan people in calling for solutions for particular untoward situations seemed to say that the time was ripe for some changes in the social structures and ways of thinking that could correct the problems and repaint the big picture that was not working well.

My own suggestion at the end of my last book, *The Rise and Fall of the Christian Myth* (Yale, 2017), a conclusion that drew upon the experience of the northern European nations, was to continue working toward a multicultural social democracy. Then came Trump, White Supremacy, Nationalism, Racism, Nuclear War buttons, and a picture of America's Greatness that is actually historically wrongheaded, morally egregious, and absolutely dangerous for the future of human life on planet earth. Because the Trump cabal and electorate did "win" the election, the Trump scenario has indicated to me that I must have been mistaken about the model of society upon which we had been working, that my big picture theory was too idealistic, or that the social interests that have developed in the Western nations have gotten so far out of hand that our government has not been able to control them, and that that has become part of the problem. The single issue ideology of the Tea Party Republicans that helped put Trump in office, the unthinking mantras of "greatness again" on the part of a gerrymandered and culturally deprived electorate, and his own adolescent psychology that has used the office of the President of the United States as the platform for a Fox News performance, have eroded what I thought were the traditional standards of seriousness, thoughtfulness, and political decorum in Washington and throughout the land. Instead we have what the writers for *The New York Times* have begun calling 1) a trashy and dishonest discourse about matters most personal, private, and disgusting, and 2) political rhetorics that are dishonest, deceptive, and cynical. There is apparently no concept of America as a society and government to call upon for a deliberate and reasoned discussion about policies of importance for social well-being in today's troubled world. I must have been wrong to assume that such a concept was still there and needed to be there in order to keep our social, family, and human values in view and give our political enterprise signficance. The editors and writers for *The Guardian, The Washington Post, The New York Times, Los Angeles Times, The Nation, The New Yorker, The Atlantic*, and many other literary media are now writing analytical articles in the genre of "What Went Wrong?"

Critical Times for America

That, of course, is a much better way of responding to the situation than allowing the mood of anger, anguish about the violence that has erupted, or threats of endings to human history and the planet to provide the topics for analysis and explanation. My own sense of the problem is that, if we are looking for agents and events to blame, there is not a single cause for the current confusions over politics and power in America. It is the buildup of the pursuits of self-interest on the part of the many organizations and individuals in power that now conflict with one another in the world of deregulation. The energies unleashed in America as the country where the individual (and corporation) is free to follow its own pursuits without government control have produced a society that does not want or see the need for regulation because it does not have a picture of a society that has a meaningful social value in which to live.

The overriding problem is that we still have the model of Western monarchies in mind to think about the formal structures of society. And we still have the basic outline of the Christian myth tucked away in our collective imaginations as the self-evident logic to use when thinking about moral and ethical issues. Both of these pictures are merged together in the Western mind as a mythic mentality that allows us to take the model for granted without conscious articulation or criticism. The narrative logic of the Christian myth for thinking dialectically, and the power of the monarch for executing social policies, have structured our large scale gameboard. The gameboard is structured in the mythic imagination and mentality as the platform on which the moves of corporate and federal competitions play out without having to acknowledge the underlying motivations in play and/or the consequences of the moves for the society as a whole. And yet, despite this lack of self-consciousness about the relation of the mythic (often unconscious) game board to the structure and well-being of the society as a whole, the picture of the social enterprise and its grammar (or way of reasoning) can still be violated surreptitiously by people like Trump for keeping track of "winners" and "losers" in the pursuit of success and conquest. Winning is the way we think about greatness, and the military model that kicks in at the political level has become automatic as the mental and practical mechanism for thinking about the defense of the nation. Unfortunately, this part of the overarching mentality encourages us to think about solving all problems by means of exterminating the opponents and enemies at hand. These and other intellectual grammars that have come to reside in our mythic mentality provide us with the sense-making and language we

Introduction

use to understand and talk about a current situation or state of affairs. My thesis has been that the thoughts and language common to our culture were once rooted in the narrative logic of the Christian myth, and that the social logic of that myth has not been able to engage or reflect upon the modern world with its problems, tensions, and conflicts. Examples would be the way in which the term *multicultural* has come to be used as a thoroughly negative characteristic of a progressive ideology, and the way in which the term *evil* is now used to castigate opponents and "terrorists" as if it were not possible to understand why they have done what they did, and that it calls for "exterminating" them. The other side of "evil" is "righteousness," the language sometimes used to justify our designs in the battle for control of situations, peoples, federal policies, and global economies.

We need to find some way to repaint the picture of today's world so that it can mark the human histories and values that make living together worthwhile. The stories of conflict, power, and violence that now are used to celebrate the glory of leaders as strong men and heroes who win at war no longer help. To imagine a pluralistic society at work creating a common culture of well-being may not be possible at this time, but such a picture could be a marvelous painting, and there is not really any reason to think it impossible before we try. The picture of Christendom that we do still have vaguely in mind, and the fantasy of the American Empire that has arisen in its place, do not provide us with the outlines for a common-good multicultural picture. And since we no longer have a picture of ourselves as the world within which to investigate the critical social issues that have evolved, there is some work to do in sorting through the figures, features, and clichés of the traditional pictures, the mythic and the historical, as a way to analyze the society that has devolved around us. Sorting through these social features of our history will also involve exploring our mentality in order to ask about the reasons its narrative features had for being there in the first place, and whether those reasons are still necessary considerations for the new arrangements we need in order to make living together workable in the present time. That is because the present situation is the result of our own history of inventions, glorious in their own way as human labors and achievements. But since they all have become streams of activities that are now out of hand in the modern configurations of energies and ideas in which we are presently living, we need to analyze what the concept of the social has included in our history and whether we can still imagine a society that might work without violence.

Critical Times for America

From among the many features of the structures of the societies we have constructed throughout history and still seem to have in mind, I have chosen: (1) an executive leader to whom the people have ascribed power, (2) a society that provides a forum or congress for policy deliberation, (3) congressional representatives of an educated people, (4) the role of race and racial tradition in the identification of a people and a nation, (5) the effect of an intellectual class in the ongoing analysis and cultivation of human values and histories, (6) the current situation of violence and anger and its justification as "natural" to our species, and (7) the arguments for capitalism that keep us from common good deliberations. But then it will be possible to say something about the big picture that is in the process of being painted. It is (8) the picture of a multicultural social democracy. All of these topics will be in mind in the course of the chapters that follow. None will be explored as the topic of a chapter of its own. Another development will be followed in the attempt to prepare us for the task at hand, namely, to begin the process of "painting" a big picture of a multicultural social democracy. The book is intended to make a contribution to the conversations now in process in the public domain about finding a constructive place for America in the world of nations.

I

Monarchy and Madness
The Quest for a Principle of Authority

In 1948 three professors of history at Yale University published a college textbook called *The Quest for a Principle of Authority in Europe 1715–Present*. It contained selected citations from intellectuals, journalists, and political leaders of the time from all of the European nations. It was organized by nations or regions of Europe on the one hand, and according to their histories that played out during these 233 years on the other. It was a momentous period of Western history in which *The Quest* had to deal with the breakdown of the big picture of Western civilization that had been provided by Catholic Christianity and the Roman Empires. The break up of the Empire into the many European nations which were now on their own as petty kingdoms no longer had the erstwhile overarching authorities of Christendom and its empires. The textbook was published by Holt, Rinehart and Winston as a workbook for college courses in sociology, and the authors provided introductions, commentaries, and questions for the students. At the time this book appeared it was marked as somewhat *avant garde*, given the questions about America and Europe that had been raised by the First and Second World Wars and about sociology as an academic discipline which was somewhat new to American colleges. That it came out as a book conceived by historians interested in the social issues manifest in the European histories was a strikingly relevant response to the political and intellectual atmosphere left in America by the war. I have found that their selection of issues and texts is still of value for understanding our current circumstances.

As for the term *principle of authority* in the title of the book, I am afraid we may not be able to do it full justice. The term is hardly in evidence in the eighteenth- and nineteenth-century texts. Thus it must refer to the topic the editors-authors themselves thought appropriate for their study. Reading closely, however, the term was used innocently enough, without expressly noting the cleverness and ambiguity of its several connotations. Authority was clearly related in the minds of the professors to the authors and ideas presented in the literatures they cited, and in that context it still could have its primary connotation to intellectuals as authors and authorities. In the tradition of literary criticism, the analysis of the intention of an author had become important as a way to understand a writing in the "historical" setting of the author and its concerns. The Yale historians did not comment on this academic rubric as one of the reasons for using the term *authority*, but they were very much focused on the intentions of the speehes, literary essays, and compositions they cited for each "problem" as they asked about the quest for a principle of (*political*) authority. One has to read the instructions to their student-readers to see that these historians were aware of the double connotation of the term even while using it to cover for a concept of society toward which they thought Europe was moving, namely toward a social democracy. If we put this together with the list of ideologies that governed the European quest, we can see that the underlying assumption was that it was both the social office and the *ideas* about social formations that surfaced in the quest for "principles" that interested these professors. A reading of the Table of Contents reveals that the principles under review ran from the Enlightenment (where individuals were asked to think about their place in the history of their nation, e.g., Voltaire), and *liberalism* (a term used to characterize the views of authors addressing the dissolution of governments and the need for societies to craft their own, such as Locke, Voltaire, Montesquieu, Adam Smith, and Condorcet), through monarchy, nationality, ethnicity, and country, to democracy, fascisim, communism, and social democracy. None of these "principles" are discussed as alternative conceptual theories of society, but all are treated as concepts and ideologies of some conscious importance for the peoples involved, and most have major political figures and events marking the differences they made for their histories. It is a marvelous survey of this momentous period of Western Civilization troubled by the end of Christendom and enaging in a quest for a new principle and concept of society now that the model of Christian monarchy was no longer working.

The eighteenth and nineteenth centuries were filled with various attempts by intellectuals and authors to combine "liberalism" (from the French revolution) with "nationalism" (the vague sense of identity left over from the petty kingdoms) by struggling with features of the monarchies still remembered and somehow still extant within a given nation. Examples would be the writings of Bolingbroke, Goethe, Rousseau, and von Herder. But at the end of the eighteenth century it was the French Revolution that turned ideas into actions and actually brought down a monarchy. The ideas of *liberté, eqalité*, and *fraternité* generated more than a revolution. They became slogans to justify the many experiments and inventions of new social constructions in France and throughout Europe for the next century. The model of monarchy did not easily go away. It was always in mind as the traditional form of government that had assured stability, order, and regular patterns of trade and diplomacy. But during the eighteenth century most dynasties finally came to an end of some kind, and the concepts of a constitution and laws took the place of the king in the quest for a principle of authority. The problem was that it had been the will of the king as a person, not a written constitution or set of laws, that gave the traditional monarchy and its nation a sense of authority and order. Without a royal figure to represent authority, and without a customary way for a nation to devise another constitution and write a set of laws, a vacancy in leadership, authority, and the customary shape of society opened up. Political activists and thinkers had to work without traditional credentials in efforts to unite the people with their own proposals aimed at retaining the concept of the nation. Then, in the middle of the century Karl Marx published his *Communist Manifesto*, which analyzed the conditions of the working class in the developing industrial economies, and, as some intellectuals have interpreted it, called for structural changes to address the subjugation of the workers by the capitalistic systems of industry. This publication was widely read and produced several schools of social thought as efforts in calling for structural changes to the familiar patterns of a given society. One effect took place in Russia under Trotsky, Lenin, and Stalin where the attempt was made to build a common good nation by using the police and the military to disband the aristocracy, make capitalism illegal, and force the peasantry to labor in communes. Another effect took place in Italy under Mussolini. It does not appear to have been as ruthless as the Russian experiment at the level of its demands upon the people, but at the level of theory it was much more radical and drastic. It was Mussolini who coined the term *fascism* (from *fascis*, a bundle of wooden rods surrounding a metal hook) to serve as a sign and symbol for the way the authorities (soon to be dictators) had to treat the people as if by flogging in order to demand obedience from them and control the state.[1] One can see that the concepts of *liberté* ("freedom," "liberalism") and democracy had already gone too far in the minds of "rulers" such as Stalin and Mussolini. They were simply unable to understand and appreciate the general European restlessness among the people under military and authoritarian control. In their minds it was power to the ruler, not power to the people that was called for in order to make a society work.

The new leaders were, of course, trying hard to address the confused conditions caused by the break up and erosion of the European empires and monarchies. But they did not have social histories sufficient to tell them how to go about creating a government for a society that would work by and for the people in the post-monarchy times. The best they could do, they thought, was to ward off the unrest of the proletariate and make sure the workers were cared for by the government as best the government could. In their view, the people as an uneducated mass could not do so for themselves. These rulers were not the only experimenters of the century, to be sure, but their turn to military force as the practical exigency thought necessary to assure that their "authority" was effective has become the example of the failure of Western mentality in crisis, an example of the reach for authority and power in the hands of a single ruler whose self-interests in personal power and authority actually compete with those of the society to determine policy instead of allowing concern for the well-being of a democratic society to take the lead.

There were also, fortunately, many others: the Jacobins in France, Jeremy Bentham in England, von Humbolt and von Bismarck in Germany (Prussia), and many others at work on the problem of imagining human society anew without a king, all deeply exercised by the untoward consequences of the French Revolution and the subsequent period of Napoleon and his armies. Alas. Although there were huge investments in political

---

1. The terms "bundle" and "axe" are correct, at least in terms of modern translations. It should be clear, however, that Mussolini did not invent the term *fascis* itself. The term comes from the Etruscans and is loaded with myriad usages and connotations throughout Roman and Italian history. A "bundle of sticks surrounding a hook" used for "flogging" is also an accurate picture. *Fascis* likewise connotes punitive usage by guards in a palace, etc. So Mussolini did not "coin" the term, but he was the one who picked it up and turned it into a political party definition.

Monarchy and Madness

experiments and next-step progams, they did not eventuate in any common agreement about a workable democracy that could serve as an alternative to monarchy, military regime and fascism. Russia centered on state-run communism, thinking that the concept of socialism itself would evolve automatically into a fully orbed society in support of meaning and morality sufficient to celebrate the human need and penchant for stability and community. That did not happen. Italy ended up being against both socialism and communism, thinking that, because Rome was the center of the older Roman Empire, Italy could mark the turn to fascist leadership in Europe on the model of empire. That did not happen. France was a veritable hot bed of democratic and intellectual activists, but was not able to constrain those who still wanted a monarchy (e.g. the Vichies). And Germany, a large group of petty kingdoms without unity during the entire nineteenth century was forced again and again to consider this arrangement and that, but without success. There was the invigorating political scene of Prussia during the first decades of the nineteenth century with intellectuals such as von Humbolt calling for a Constitution, and the edict of Frederick William, the king, on the End of Serfdom; the Frankfort Assembly (1848) calling for the unity of the German princedoms and offering Frederick the crown which he rejected; Bismarck's call for becoming an empire (The Imperial Proclamation, 1871); the Pan-German League (1891–98); the Weimar Republic (1919–32); and Hitler's organization of the National Socialist Workers' Party (1919). The tussle between Protestants (Prussia) and Catholics (Vienna) also played an unsettling role. And when Hitler took advantage of the ill-considered Treaty of Versailles after the First World War to espouse his notion of ethnic purity and military power as the only way to end the German resentments and guarantee a glorious future for Germans and Germany, the stage was set for the Nazis; the slaughter of six million Jews and about six million others labeled as undesirables—Russians, Poles, Romani, Freemasons, and homosexuals; and the Second World War.

If we discount for a moment the horrors of fascism that developed, we can look back and appreciate the responses of the petty European kingdoms left to their own devices by the devolution of Christendom, empires, monarchies, and feudalism. They can be appreciated as marvelous if faulty attempts for people without power to think through a brand new social circumstance: people without a king. They worked with the Western traditions of societies, social institutions, histories, attitudes, and logics to attempt a rationale for a new social formation (a modern nation-state this side of the French discovery of democracy). Note the number of categories that were taken for granted throughout this century as component elements of what they understood to be the features of a "nation": racial extraction (French, Italian, German, English, Polish, etc.), country (land), leaders (intellectuals, politicians), rulers (erstwhile monarchs, generals), traditions (history), religions, and law. Most of these features of social formation had been around for ages in one configuration or another since tribalism. One could think of this list of social features as the basic components for the many creative and constructive social formations in the Western history of the human race. One might think that these resources should have been enough for the post Christendom puzzle to be creatively rearranged. But, unfortunately, there was little awareness of the importance of cultural mentality as a social logic that gave a people its ethos and sense of identity. And there were other items that had been added to the list, such as the "need" for an army, that frequently got in the way of resolving conflicts between and among princedoms and nations as the experiments unfolded. They did not realize that this older pattern of force and aggression would soon be counterproductive within a capitalistic and technological global age. And although other components, such as religions and cultures were on the list of national characteristics, religion and culture did not count as resources of importance for thinking clearly about the values and morals needed for the shape and mentality of a new social formation.

It is also terribly unfortunate, though explainable, that these Europeans had no picture of an alternative multicultural society, the values of which might have suggested more meaningful and celebrative ways to experience and cultivate alternatives to Christendom, "empires," "kingdoms," and even "confederations." The perceived intellectual problems in every case were the new concepts of "liberalism" and "democracy," the very concepts needed, not only to "solve" the problem of imagining a post-Christendom, post-monarchy society, but also to begin imagining a society much more colorful, workable, and interesting than any of those in the past or proposed by the nineteenth-century intellectuals for their nations' futures. The question is how that could have been. At least since the era of colonialism, the world was known to be full of different peoples and their cultures. Normal human curiosity about another people should have been enough for a stop at the border, hat in hand, to ask to have some conversations about one another's differences and projects, as well as common rewards for learning how to get along. But the mental residue of Christian mentality determined that the

Western logic of the "us and them," a distinction of difference very close to right and wrong, or superior and inferior (Christian or "pagan"), left little room for thinking about other cultures as interesting and authentic. And the driving force of the colonialism that was in the process of developing was not curiosity or intrigue about another people's culture, but trade, expansion of territory, conquest, and exploitation. Thus the self-interests of an expanding capitalistic enterprise left little time for interest in other kinds of engagements with cultures of difference.

This means that the quest for a "principle of authority" in eighteenth- to twentieth-century Europe was not able to name one principle, if ever there was such a "principle" to be found, or such a "quest" to be conscious and acknowledged. What can be learned from such a review of our history is that the very notion of a "principle of authority," though helpful as an academic topic, is archaic as an historical descriptive. It evokes a very long history of the aristocratic empires of the ancient Near East, and the Christian addition of an all-powerful deity at the top of a hierarchy of priests, kings, and popes, a deity who rules both the cosmos and history, the Christian "kingdom" and the world. This location of a mythic "principle" of "authority" that gave rationale to the Western history of empires was not acknowledged as part of the past tradition that had to be reevaluated for the modern European history. Nevertheless, we can learn many things from this review of the recent chapter of Western civilization. One was that the kings of the petty kingdoms were not able to imagine their kingdoms as a society that organized for freedom and democracy. Another is that individuals arising from the proletariate or from the aristocracy to a position of leadership and power (as if "kings") had a difficult time convincing the people of their right and ability to care for the welfare of their nation. A third is that the military option to force order was mostly automatic but functioned most awkwardly and was ineffective in its many applications. And a fourth is that the image of a powerful leader as the only way to shape and control a nation resulted in dictatorships, if not fascism.

It is the ease with which the would-be-powerful leaders in Italy, Germany, and Russia fell into fascism that marks this century as a frightful lesson that we, the people, have not yet learned to confront. The fall into fascism was not recognized as a feature of the breakdown of the mono-cultural Western tradition that left the erstwhile centers of divine power and royal authority vacant, thus allowing for attempts by strong men to revert to national power by means of personal authority. The vacancy of divine and royal authority should have called for critical analysis of the human phenomenon of social formation, mythmaking, and culture on the part of intellectuals and culture critics. That in a sense is what happened during this period without realizing it. But the underlying problem of Christendom's mentality, still at work as a residual model for social formations, was based on a mythic world view that resisted critical analysis and did not provide concepts ready at hand to understand and analyze the social situations that developed as it passed away. Thus the fall into fascism was into an intellectual and social vacancy where only the vaguest suggestions were still discernable of what it would take to repair the social fragmentation and keep civilization alive and healthy.

The fascists did find a number of rubrics for their projects, of course: a single party "politics," a single ruler with absolute executive power, a military backup to guarantee "obedience," and a nation cleansed of all confusion and uncleanness, including democrats, subversives, immigrants, and the Jews. The fascists' visions of a majestic Italy, a great and pure Germany, and a powerful communist Russia were clearly articulated as ideals by using features taken from their own Christian histories, now combined with more recent collective concepts drawn from the French Revolution and Karl Marx. But then the ugliness of untoward events began to take place such as the massacre of the Jews in Germany, the slaughter of opponents in Russia, and the results of the indigenization of farmers in the communes. The peoples hardly knew what to make of it. There were, of course, many "protests" such as the myriad attempts at the rural and local levels in Russia to take back their products and property from the commissars, and the flights of the Jews and intellectuals from Vienna before the *Anschluss* by Hitler. Alas. In every case, the grandeur of the pictures their "leaders" projected for their nations and their own powers was not enough to prevail. They became, in fact, grotesque. Millions were massacred revealing the horror possible when social and political power falls into the hands of ego centric "leaders." There has to be a shared concept of a society as a community for the well-being of the people and nation to guard against such individuals and make possible the emerging values of social democracy with its representative councils instead of totalitarian dictators. In the Western tradition, a totalitarian state can only lead to destruction.

This review of the European quest up until the Second World War, even though it has worked with the emergence of fascists as a special problem for modern social democracies, has not introduced the concept of *individualism* that helped make the fascists possible, and that will play a central role in the histories of the United States in the next chapter. It is therefore time to explore the roots of the concept in the history of Western Christianity. The Christian picture of the cosmos (or universe), which was the mythic world for Christendom, provided the setting for all the social formations of the Christian empire, and the self-understandings for all those with particular roles in the society. These roles included the functions of the all-powerful deity at the top of the world, the monarchs at the top of the hierarchies of power in the kingdoms and empires below, the pope at the pinnacle of religious authority in the institution of the church, the priests and nuns with responsibility for the rituals of the church and its monasteries, and the aristocrats in their feudal estates. *Power* was the primary characteristic of these offices and officers in the workings of the society. If we think of them as persons, none of them needed to be socialized with partners and forums that had the capacity to manage even a sector of the society or experiment with new ideas and discussions about the structure of society, much less the meaning of social existence. The mythic world was set, and that was all that was needed to call for the meaningful performance of a particular role. And the paradigm for meaningful performance was the deity in the highest, the image of singular existence and absolute power. Now that Christendom was fractured, the sense of power and authority located in one of the traditional rulers was gone. It was only the mythic paradigm that the fascists unconsciously sought to fulfill.

As for the Jesus Christ part of the myth, and his father god in the heavens, for more than a thousand years scholars have had fun working over the biblical and other texts looking for the "reasons" why this "Old Testament" deity did not have a "consort" just as some other cultural myths of the time had. Answers to the "why" questions of mythic figures and narratives are simply not the way a troublesome myth can be questioned, corrected, or polished. The "reasons" for a mythic image have little to do with its narrative logic in its own mythic world. They are given with the social logic of the society and its people who have used the myth to articulate and confirm the patterns of their own social structures. And so it was that the patriarchal social formations of the ancient Near Eastern societies, especially in their Hebrew formations, produced myths that assumed male leadership in the cosmos above, and in all of the roles responsible for the structure and function of institutions and society on earth below.

Critical Times for America

Once the Jesus people tacked themselves on to the history of the Hebrews and created the Bible with its Old and New "Testaments," they had a problem with the way to imagine the relationship of the Hebrew God to their new deity, especially since the mythic worlds of the Greco-Roman period within which they found themselves, and with which they had to do their thinking about finding their place as a new religion and social formation, were full of stories about human heroes ascending to their places in the cosmic orders of "divine" agency and power, a divine world full of family relationships among the gods. Thus the closest relations imaginable were two: that Jesus become one of these cosmic powers, and that he be recognized as the "son" of the highest god his "father." The first was made imaginable in the so-called "Christ myth" where Jesus as the *christos* is crucified (by the Romans), then resurrected by God to ascend into heaven and become its ruler (1 Cor 15:3–8; Heb 1:1–4). The second relation (sonship) is even more tricky and took the early Christians a bit longer to work it out. It can be found in the logic of the stories of the "virgin birth" in the gospels, a story that later theologians cleverly refined as the "immaculate conception." That was as close as the "father" god could be imagined to have produced a "son" to be his representative in charge of a particular people on earth and its history. And so it was that the worldview of Christendom and its social psychology assumed the authority of a single male figure as the way to organize and govern its social formations.

It would be possible to analyze other indications of attempts to recognize the female in the stories, rituals, and offices of the Catholic church. Most are wonderfully humanizing and can be honored and appreciated as a kind of intellectual awareness of the limits of its male orientation to a social anthropology that should also be able to posit, place, and understand the role of the female in the human race. Alas, the notions of absolute singularity, absolute power, and "productive" ("creative") achievement in the hands of a male agent determined that the male person find its significance in the replications of that role. Unfortunately, we are not (yet?) able to study the personal and social psychology of an historical era and its religion in order to be clearer about the significance of the male figure in Western civilization. We can, however, notice the ways in which male individuals broke through the boundaries of Christendom's cosmos and produced a picture of humans standing over against the divine. A primary early example is the person of Saint Augustine of Hippo (fourth century) who wrote his *Confessions* as a conversation with God to say that he had to struggle to accept his sense of "salvation." This opened up the possibility of personal and individual self-awareness right at the point of reflection about one's relation to the power that pervaded the mythic world of the cosmos. It also introduced a new genre of literature in which the mythic world became the background for personal essays. In the case of Francesco Petrarch, the fourteenth-century founder of European Humanism, the shift in worldview was from the mythic world of the divine agencies above, with which all pious persons should have been completely preoccupied, to the beauties of the valleys on earth below when viewed from the mountain top (probably Mont Ventoux, France). In his *Secretum meum*, a set of three dialogues Petrarch held with Augustine in the presence of the personification of Truth, he tells how overwhelmed he was with the beauty of the natural landscape, and that he felt guilty to find the earthly realm as lovely as the spiritual realm of the divine. This was his experience of "the fall," and he takes from his pocket Augustine's *Confessions* where he reads Augustine's mention of men who "go to admire the high mountains and the immensity of the ocean and the course of the heavens . . . and neglect themselves." These and other reports of intellectuals were stations on the way to the discovery of the *individual* and the *natural order*, a discovery that was destined to shape the social interests of the subsequent history of human intellectual and scientific endeavors, and the self-consciousness of individual persons. It was a shift from mythic world to natural world, and from theology to anthropology as intellectual grammars. The subsequent history of scientists and their battle for rational knowledge of the human and natural orders is full of other brave and clever intellectuals such as Copernicus, Michael Montaigne, Galileo, and Newton, all of whom stepped out from the Christian mythic universe in order to explore the natural orders as the home for human existence and self-understanding.

It was, however, the Protestant Reformation that introduced another shift in the concept and self-understanding of the individual, a shift that took place *within* the context of the Catholic world. It was not a matter of stepping outside its mythic universe to explore the world of nature scientifically, as were the examples of the scientists. It was more a matter of exploring the limits of Catholic Christianity for an understanding of the social circumstances that emerged in the course of the Renaissance and Age of Discovery. The Reformation was a product of the pressure on Christendom occasioned by the expansion of the several worlds of intellectual horizons (in the Renaissance), social interests (in the Age of Discovery), enterprises such as industry, trading, and conquest that had begun, and the encounters with other peoples that occurred during the fifteenth and sixteenth centuries. Two traditions of "reformation" played a truly historic role, the one stemming from Martin Luther in the German and north European countries, and the one generated by John Calvin in Geneva Switzerland that influenced the French Huguenots and the Yankees later in England and America. Both reformation traditions played a role in the development of the Western concepts of society and the individual, but in slightly different ways. In Calvin's *Institutes of the Christian Religion*, and his restructuring of Geneva on the model of the early Christian church in the New Testament, the concept of a Christian society was developed as an answer to the demise of the Catholic Church and Christendom. The *city* was to be a kingdom of righteousness according to *biblical ethic*, and the individual was now seen to be a citizen of the city with knowledge of the Bible as its charter. In the next chapter, Colin Woodard will explain how important these Calvinists were in the formation of Yankeedom (his term) in New England, one of the eleven "nations" in America, and how important Yankeedom has been for the political history of the United States. Yankees were individuals who did not want or need the supervision or help from statist governments to tell them how to care for their cities.

In Luther's sermons and *Theses* the protest was more about the piety of the Catholic rituals of ordination, confession, and absolution as the primary function of the priesthood and how the social world looked through the eyes of this priesthood. Both reformers had focused on the Bible as a historical document that provided for the definition of Christianity at its beginning, and thus a way to question the practices of Catholicism which came later. The Bible had served Christendom as its epic history, book of ritual readings, and collection of theological literature for homilies and instruction in the teachings of the church. Its Hebrew and Greek writings had been translated into Latin from at least the fifth century (St. Jerome's *Vulgate*) and was finally made the official canon of the Catholic Church at the Council of Trent (1546), a Catholic response to the Protestants' emphasis on the Bible. The Renaissance became the occasion for other translations such as John Wycliffe's English translation (fourteenth century), William Tyndale's English Bible (1525), and Martin Luther's German translation (1534). During the Enlightenment an interest in "history" and the Greek "classical tradition" influenced scholarship on the Bible. It was now seen as the *historical* documentation for the origins of the Christian religion.

Luther's translation of the Bible into German became the official Bible within the many Lutheran traditions of Northern Europe.

Calvin used the New Testament to document the early Christian community and its practices. Luther read the New Testament as the documentation for the *kerygma*, the proclamation of the Christ myth that called for personal belief. Both were intellectuals in the Western tradition taking advantage of the invigorating circumstances created by the Renaissance and the new horizons of the Age of Discovery (in the Americas). And both were successful in their reformations of Catholicism in the founding of Christian churches that cultivated independent identities and replicated themselves to form their own religious traditions. Calvin substituted the city of Geneva for the capitals and monarchies of Christendom; Luther substituted the sermon from the Bible for the rituals of Catholicism. Both worked well at the level of conceptualizing protestant Christianity as a social institution, but of course they were not able to match the scope and comprehension of the Catholic control of the church and its empires. The Protestant churches were taking their place as religious institutions within countries and peoples that no longer had their kings or a single coherent government. Calvinism was somehow content to be an example of the Christian society in the midst of the larger social world that was now becoming "secular." Luther had developed the concept of the "two kingdoms," one for the heavenly kingdom of God, which was left in place and still in mind, and one for the earthly kingdom of human society in which Christians now lived as a kind of social conscience. When Protestants found themselves intermingling with that larger world and wondering about their identity as individual Christians deprived of the erstwhile context and authority of Catholicism, Calvin's answer from the *Institutes* was not to worry because they were the "elect" and so "predestined" for rescue from the world at its apocalyptic ending. The Lutherans did not have that problem but they did have to be careful to make sure that they were true believers in the Bible. In both cases it was the individual who now was responsible to experience belief, manifest virtue, and be sure that they were saved. That intellectual conundrum energized both the Calvinists and the Lutherans to work out their understandings both of personal "salvation" and of the Christian's proper engagement of the social world.

It was Max Weber who analyzed this problem in the nineteenth century as the question of the relation between one's faith and one's energies devoted to economic success in the world of industry, a feature that was particularly characteristic of Protestants. He started with the observation that the protestant individual was responsible for making sure of one's own belief and salvation. He theorized that the uncertainty about one's "salvation" created the need to "prove" one's election in the way one lived in the social world. This was then a primary motivation for the Protestant Ethic and the protestant acceptance of the capitalism that was just then emerging as a concept of importance for the societies that had been left to their own devices in the ending of Christendom. Western culture had devolved upon the self-understanding of the individual.

The "quest" we have had in view for a "Principle of Authority" did not pay any special attention to the Protestants as the way in which Western culture may have still been influential in the political chaos of the eighteenth and nineteenth centuries. And since Catholicism did not just dry up and blow away, there were now three major Christian traditions alive and well during the period when the "Quest for a Principle of Authority" was under way. At the level of political struggle to form governments, the effect of different religions was hardly noticed except when a conflict arose in one of the cities that appealed to one of the religions, as in France and England where religions became important for labeling political movements and served as ideologies. Ideologies played their part in the struggle mainly as labels, not as mythic grammars or social logics that had some hold upon the identity and self-understanding of a people. People continued to identify themselves in terms of ethnic traditions and were forced now to think in terms of governments. As we have seen, the term that became common was "nation," and the quest was for a nation's "constitution," rationale, and political authority. Lacking a clear answer to these questions, the vacancy left by the demise of both Christendom and the kings was available for non-credentialed would-be rulers to step forward. This was possible in the confusion of authorities and the emerging awareness of individualism and political power. The remarkable thing about this development is that each of the many individuals claiming leadership had to justify their claim by marshalling not the people (as in a democracy), but some current ideology or feature of their people's ethnic tradition. Thus Mussolini called upon the history of Rome and the Romans; Hitler the racial purity of the Germans; Stalin the Marxist (Communist) utopia. And the strange thing about all of these examples and others of the time is that the projection of such a vision was enough to keep the people quiet and gather an army around the visionary. I need not draw the analogy to the current President of the

United States at this point. The features of similarity and their historical connections will have to wait for another chapter.

We should, however, notice that the review of the European configurations by our Yale professors did not find the "principle of authority" they were looking for in the European history. They did call the reader's attention to their own answer to the quest at the end of the textbook, and that answer was that, even though there was not yet a clear "principle of authority," the history's trend was toward the formation of a social democracy as the answer to the quest. There is some reason to agree with this reading of the "trend," except that it leaves out the critical period of the two World Wars. It was the wars that brought to focus the failures of the chaotic quest period and provided a postwar platform for starting over with a fresh roster of leaders, such as Konrad Adenauer and Helmut Kohl in Germany and Clement Atlee in England. With the help of America's Marshal Plan the European Nations became *Nation-States*, and the Nation-States found themselves drawn together as a European Community. There was the Treaty of Paris (1951), the European Community (1952), the Maastricht Treaty (1992), and other conferences that charted the work of coming to agreement for the *European Union* (1993). It was only in the process of this truly historic moment for the Western Tradition of civilization that the social democratic structures of nation-states developed. And the creation of workable social democracies was only possible on the way to the conception and execution of a workable coalescence or *union* of states. Since the Second World War the European Union and the United Nations have created frameworks that are truly *avant-garde* and promising for addressing social issues. The principles of freedom and democracy had been taken seriously, and the principles of law, welfare, and common good were no longer thought to be obstacles, but necessary for a modern nation and people. All of this has happened with the horrible histories of the totalitarian states serving as haunting reminders of just how serious the quest for a social democracy is, and how necessary it has become for the nation states within a common region, tradition, or culture to agree to work together in the interests of having social democracies.

We might want to include the United States in the list of socially creative "unions" of nation-states except for the fact that it was not a response to the history of totalitarian regimes as were the European Union and the United Nations, but an unlikely formation of a Federal Union of independent colonies struggling to remain independent of the European empires

Critical Times for America

(mainly those of England, France, and Spain) that had produced them during the seventeenth and eighteenth centuries. Thus there is in America a new set of obstacles that have been causing uncertainty about the welfare of our society. One is that our concept of America as the land of the free, a concept that has been there from the beginning and that made the colonies attractive for immigrants, has evolved into a culture of individualisms that is threatened by thoughts of government control and a common good society. Another is the thought of a multicultural society as the solution to living well together in the new age of globalism. Especially in America, the scope of the vision needed for a multicultural society seems to be too large and complicated for the current American mind-set to entertain. It may be that the traditional model of public education in our nation, which consisted of an expanding series of social contexts as the "worlds" in which we have lived from the local village, through the state, to the institutions of the federal government and world at large is no longer in place. It was customary in the past to parcel this series of social worlds out to the schools most of us attended from elementary school through high school and college. Social arenas became the topics for classes in the disciplines of the arts and sciences on the way to knowledge of a culture. That has apparently been eroded by the recent complexities of social histories and the "values" that now determine our enterprises, media, and world encounters. These complexities have not been adequately acknowledged and addressed, nor do we seem to know how to go about constructing a more relevant educational system.

It is also the case that the glitches to our progress toward the promise of a multicultural social democracy recently caused by Brexit in Europe and Trump in America can be seen as symptoms of a social dis-ease this side of the history of fascism that ruined the concept of democracy in the nineteenth and twentieth centuries in Europe and that now threatens America. The main symptom at the moment is the rise of a racist nationalism that calls for very serious analysis. In the case of Trump's election, the symptoms include the way in which the electorate responded to his slogans about "greatness," a response that indicates a serious problem of low level intelligence and lack of political education in America. It is of course the case that the failure of the economy to keep pace with the needs and expectations of the people purportedly caused a general mood of grievance that Trump could provoke. But the gap between his rhetoric and his politics has meant that the working classes that supported him will not be the better for it. Trump is acting like a fascist-in-the-making. He represents the mentality of capitalism and its set of rules for the production of personal and corporate wealth at the expense of both the government and the people as a society. His own single policy mind-set is the protection of personal wealth. And the Republican party that supported him has created a single party Congress that supports the rich incorporations against the interests and welfare of the people. Democrats were hoping that the legacy of the party since Franklin Delano Roosevelt was about to wrest free from Wall Street's grip with another president like Obama whose health care programs, civil rights sensibilities, and responses to climate change, war, and global diplomacy could write the next chapter of our history. Not so. The Trump cabal of millionaires turned out to be white male supremacists, dismayed to have had a black man as president, and angry at the thought of a woman being president. The president's legislative program is mainly a set of bills and propositions designed to repeal and destroy the previous (Obama and Democratic) administrations' efforts in welfare, equality, climate change, and diplomacy. Trump and his Tea Party Republicans have absolutely no interest in the welfare of all the people. The underlying bias of white male supremacy has shown its colors in many of Trump's programs such as building a wall against Mexicans, devising immigration rules against Muslims, railing against women in politics, and targeting all of the Obama administration's achievements for repeal. We need, therefore, to devote the next chapters to the question of social identity and the quest for a multicultural social democracy in America. We need to know how it can be that a white male supremacy has surfaced in our society and penetrated our political system to the degree that the human values we once thought were basic have been crushed (Steve Bannon's term.) The social-psychological factor in view will be the combination of individualism, a fascination with absolute power, and the pursuit of wealth at the expense of the welfare of the society as a whole.

2

Nations and Races
America's History of Eleven Nations

Colin Woodard has retold the story of America in two recent publications. The popular story, which he has revised, featured the Pilgrims and Puritans in New England, the conflict with Great Britain over control of the colonies, the Boston tea party, and the revolutionary war. This war became the occasion for some internal conflicts among the colonies up and down the Atlantic coast, as well as the involvement of France and the Native American Indians in skirmishes with the Britsh navy and armed forces in the Northern territories around Lake Champlain and in the bays and harbor towns of New England and the Chesapeake. Then there was the calling of a Continental Congress and the writing of the Constitution that featured the leadership of John Hancock, Thomas Jefferson, John Adams, and others as representatives from the colonies. The thirteen colonies soon became states and the United States was born. After that there was a period in which the expansion toward the West began. Conflicts among the states about whether the new territories and states should be "slave" or "free" occasioned the Civil War. The subsequent "taking" of the West with the stories of the Lewis and Clark trail, the Indian Wars, homesteads, railroads, the Alamo, and the California gold rush rounded out the story of America as the Land of the Free "from sea to shining sea." With that as the story of America's origin and history as the United States, the modern period of industrialization could unfold. Participation in the Second World War, and the taking of our place of leadership among the nations after the war, soon marked us as the richest, most powerful nation by the end of the twentieth century. Now, of course, well into the twenty-first century this last chapter of the history has become troubled and problematic.

Woodard revises this picture in the first book, *American Nations: A History of the Eleven Rival Regional Cultures of North America* (2011), then analyzes its consequences for the *American Character* in his second book (2016), the subtitle of which is "*A History of the Epic Struggle Between Individual Liberty and the Common Good.*" The new picture he paints brings our long forgotten differences, conflicts, and wars among the colonies, and is stunningly relevant for understanding our political history and current situation. He uses the term *nation* as a way to designate eleven distinct people, their cultures, and the reasons they had for immigration to the Americas, peoples whose social formations as colonies in the "new lands" became "regions" that are not the same as the "states" we usually have in mind. He works with the European extractions of the "founders" of these colonies, the reasons for their interests in America, their rivalries as the colonies came to jockey for territory and influence in the process of becoming "states," and how they became political entities and regions with histories of their expansions, mostly to the West. This history is traced to reveal what Woodard calls the "character," others have left unnamed except for political attitudes, and I have sometimes called "mentalities." He describes how their practical purposes, ways of life, and political characteristics became attitudes informing major projects, self-understandings, and ideologies of large groups and units of people who have influenced political orientations and issues in America right up until our time. Woodard's name for it (*"The Epic Struggle between Individual Liberty and the Common Good"*) is a profound analysis of the current tussle between political parties that we have called the "red" and the "blue." I want briefly to review this history as a sequel to the European quest for a "Principle of Authority" in the last chapter, by noting the American mentalities that make our own "quest" for a principle of authority problematic in other ways. But first a simple listing of Woodard's "nations." He locates these eleven social formations and their separate histories on a map of North America from their "foundings" to their spread across the lands up until the present time. In each case there is a particular history to be told and an analysis of its influence for our collective character. The map included here will help to understand the sequence of the listings because

Critical Times for America

it highlights both the topography and the cultural orientation for a given nation's place and importance for the larger picture.

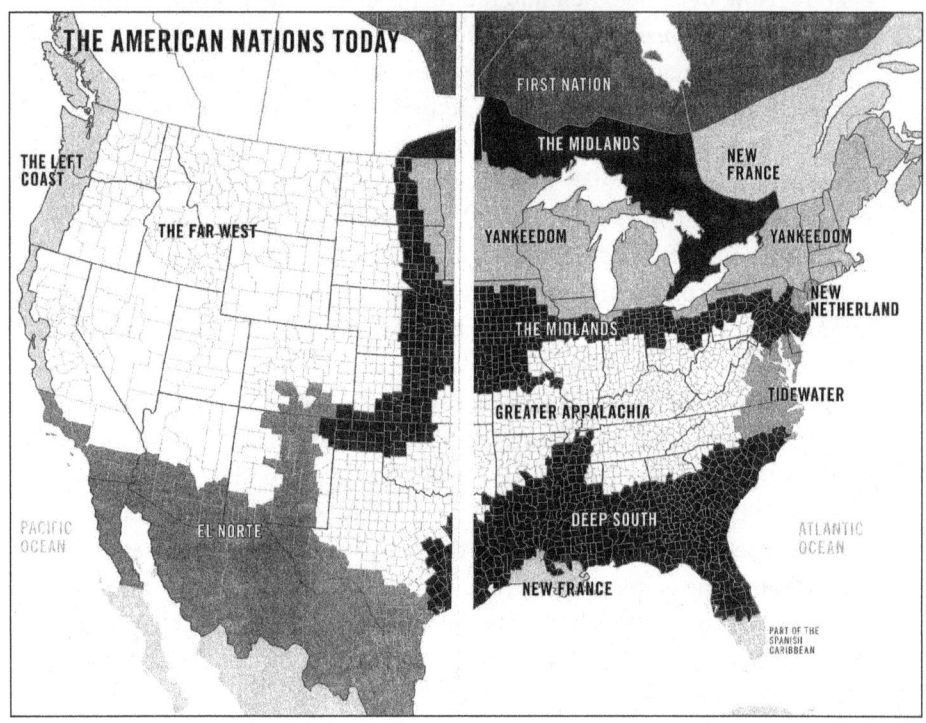

EL NORTE

Soon after the voyages of Columbus (1492), there were Spanish missions to the New World. The New World was a huge territory without geographic definition, granted to Spanish explorers and missionaries by Pope Alexander VI a century before the English landed at Jamestown on the Eastern seaboard of North America. The Pope had no idea of the size of his grant, nor that it included two gigantic continents, but Spanish explorers, missionaries, and warriors soon mapped the coastlines of both North and South America, colonized the Caribbean and middle America, and turned the Pacific Southwest into a region of posts and patrons from what is now Mexico City to Santa Fe, New Mexico, and Monterey, California. They mapped the Pacific Coast of the Oregon Country and the Canadian Maritimes They explored the Kansas prairies and the Smokey Mountains of Tennessee, and gave names to many major geological features of North America and the Coast of California as far as the Canadian Maritimes (Bay of Fundy, *Bahia*). They founded short-lived colonies on the shores of Georgia and Virginia, and the oldest European city in America (St. Augustine, Florida). The center of the culture Woodard calls El Norte was in northern New Mexico (Santa Fe) and southern Colorado long before the English immigrants came to explore the West.

When the time came for California and Oregon to join the Union during the mid nineteenth century, the El Norte culture was already entrenched. This did not become part of the popular story of the Westward Ho, probably because this story was full of the miners, fur traders and settlers from the East who had taken the trails across the Western plains and the Rockies to reach the Pacific. The *nortenos* had not become an independent state of Mexico, were already bi-cultural (Latino), did not need to fence their lands, and had little reason to think of the Native Americans as enemies. Their influence was great, however, right up into the present time. It had to do with their farming methods, their foods (rice, corn, and beans), their ranching practices, and what might be called their cowboy culture throughout the West. *Norteno* culture did not go away. It still provides the basis for California's two layered self-understanding, history, and politics.

NEW FRANCE

The French got in on the waves of immigration to the New World, landing two boat loads of immigrants at St. Croix, Maine, in 1604. After some hard knocks because of the bitter winters, their leader, Samuel de Champlain, moved them to Nova Scotia where they experimented with farming and formed a camaraderie called the "Order of Good Cheer." When the farming did not do well they sailed back up the St Lawrence river where they founded the city of Quebec (1608). They had no trouble making friends with the native Americans, whom they regarded as human beings (equals), and practiced cultural openness. Woodard names them the New France, and notes that in their later involvement with the English settlers to the South, and the developing tensions with England that produced the Revolutionary War, the people of New France found themselves caught between the French values of independence, equality, and resistance to hierarchy, on the one hand, and the fact that they had no interest in a war against the British who had made possible the fur and beaver trade all the way across the continent, and who had laid claim to the lands we now call Canada. New France did not join the United States, but because of its influence in the history of the United States, both as the Canadian Province to the north and as France's role later in the South (Florida; Louisiana), Woodard includes it in the list of "nations" that have played significant roles in the political and cultural formations of the United States.

TIDEWATER

The founding of Jamestown by the Virginia Company in 1607 brought the English aristocracy, or better the sons of the English lords and their manors, to the New World. They thought to construct a colony on the model of the English countryside, building estates, growing tobacco, farming with indentured servants, and trading with England. As British colonies they understood their lands as theirs to govern, and offered the lands toward the West to new immigrants in fifty-acre plots. For the Africans who were purchased as slaves, however, and treated as indentured servants, these lands were not available. The children of the colonists were educated at home in what was understood as the classical tradition of Greek Republicanism, then sent to England for their "higher education." The Tidewater colonists sought to inhibit, then conquer if necessary the adjacent tribes of the native Americans who got in the way. When the Revolutionary War began they were first royalists (in opposition to the Puritans), and then, having agreed with the Yankees about the need for the revolution, became the leaders of the Continental Congresses and the authors of the Constitution. Thus Hamilton, Jefferson, Adams, and others became the "fathers" of the United States.

YANKEEDOM

The northern coast of America we now call New England with its center in Boston was the region that received the Pilgrims and Puritans. They did not plan to start plantations, as in the Tidewater or the Deep South, or found a trading center, as in New Amsterdam (New York), but rather to build a new society in the new land based on Protestant readings of John Calvin and the Bible. They came as family units and founded "cities" with their churches, schools, parks, and municipal buildings. They had the Calvinist model of a theocracy and utopia in mind, just the opposite of the aristocratic organizations of the Tidewater and the Deep South.

The laws they wrote for their cities were moralistic and rather rigid in the interest of the "complete society" that Woodard calls "communitarian," not limited to matters of finance and taxation as were those of the Tidewater and the South. Their influence in the shaping of the United States was focused mainly on their vision of a communitarian society, their opposition to the Tidewater politicians, and their intellectual leadership in the formation of the civil structures of the Nation.

NEW NETHERLANDS

The city that became New York was first founded and populated by the Dutch as a trading center in 1624. The Dutch had become an independent nation in Europe under a treaty of 1579 and had developed an intellectual and cultural heritage that set it apart from the other European nations. It was the country known for the philosophies of Rene Descartes, where Galileo had his astronomies published, Spinoza's cultural histories were generated, and John Locke's "Letter Concerning Toleration" was published (1689). In America the Dutch founded New Amsterdam as a fur trading post with relations to both the Dutch East India Company (1602) and the Dutch West India Company. Though largely populated at first by Calvinist (Puritan) immigrants from Holland and Eastern England, it was soon attracting the full range of European cultural traditions: Walloons from France, Lutherans from Poland and other northern European countries, Catholics from Ireland and Portugal, Anglicans, Puritans, and Quakers from England, and Ashkenazi and Sephardic Jews from Spain. Its characteristics as a city were tolerance, openness to free inquiry, and private enterprise, the very features that would come to mark the American society of the future. But New Amsterdam had little interest in modelling or governing the larger society.

THE DEEP SOUTH

Those who colonized the deep South did not come directly from England, but from the English aristocracy of Barbados where they had created a sugar plantation oligarchy based on slave labor. It was this slave state system that the Barbadians introduced to South Carolina when they landed at Charleston to colonize North America. Charleston became a very wealthy city on the model of Bridgetown, capital of Barbados, and the colonists developed large plantations in the Carolinas, Georgia, and the lands West as far as the

Mississippi. Both sugar and cotton were labor intensive plantations, and the planters became dependent upon African slaves to work their plantations. They also kept sumptuous estates in England where they continued to cultivate their connections to the aristocracy there, and were known in England and Europe as the richest and most luxurient society in the world. In America, the plantations centered what there was of civilization in which all services such as courts, legislative bodies, schools, churches, and financial controls were fully in the hands of the oligarchy. Only the sons and daughters of the families were educated (at home), then sent to England for their "higher" education. The slaves were left uneducated and cared for on the plantation model of the oligarchy.

THE MIDLANDS

Pennsylvania was a Quaker land grant between the Tidewater and the New Netherlands. It was populated not only by a small colony of Quakers from England who wanted to be left alone on their private family farms, but, because the Quakers were tolerant of other religious traditions and not interested in forcing others to become Quakers, by other immigrants as well from Scotland, Ireland, and Germany. As a Quaker, William Penn was not interested in treating Pennsylvania as a nation with its own militia, laws, and social responsibilities. It therefore became a land open and free to others who spread out to the West to develop personal farmsteads. When caught between the Yankees to the North and the Tidewater politicians to the south in the jockeying that took place prior to and during the Revolutionary War, Philadelphia did experience some armed conflict and tried to find ways for Pennsylvania to take a position with regard to the loyalties that were at stake in all the other nations. But the people found it hard to consider taking sides in the war and became the nation that generated the experience of individal independence and anti-government. This attitude then spilled over into the Appalachian expansion that produced the individualistic can-do character of the Midlands to the West.

APPALACHIA

The area marked as Greater Appalachia was the last to be settled during the colonial period. Woodard calls the immigrants "A clan-based warrior culture from the borderlands of the British Empire." The Scots-Irish from the "borderlands" of Northern and North Eastern England, and the Germans who came without land grants, were mostly poor and bedraggled from centuries of inter-tribal warfare, fleeing the impossible conditions of England during the first half of the eighteenth century. They landed in several places along the Northern seacoast, but mainly in Pennsylvania where the Quakers received them without question. They eagerly moved through Pennsylvania and its wooded, mountainous landscape to its Western and Southern borders, forming encampments and small villages, then down the Appalachian Trail to the South, cutting off the opportunity for Tidewater to expand West. They had little sense of community except for clan connections, and no sense of government. They were "proud, independent, and disturbingly violent," according to Woodard, and became a disruptive element there on the edges of the Midlands, Tidewater, and the Deep South during the period before and during the Revolutionary War. They did not want any other authority to govern them. When they learned about the other states' desire for them to become a state they responded by violent resistance and attacks on all the obvious institutions that had been built by other settlers as well as on the indigenous Indian tribes. Their occasional destruction of forts, churches, and other encampments took place on the way to a major attack against the state-house in Philadelphia which caused consternation throughout the colonies and resulted in a few agreements with their neighboring colonies about their grievances. Their anti-government individualism became a major factor in the subsequent political history of the United States.

THE FAR WEST

After the Revolutionary War the lands to the West provided for the expansion of the colonial nations and the challenges of creating homesteads, new cities, and industries. These lands also became the occasion for fierce battles in the creation of new states and the decisions as to whether they would be (could be) "slave states," as the Deep South wanted, or "free" as the Yankees wanted. That story worked its way out through the Missouri Compromise, the Lincoln-Douglas debates, the presidential campaign of 1860, the secession of South Carolina, and the Civil War. By this time all of the colonial Nations, except New Netherlands and the Tidewater, had expanded to the West but only as far as the hundredth meridian running north and south through the middle of the Dakotas, Nebraska, and Kansas. That left the

Plains, the Rocky Mountains, and the Western lands as far as the Pacific Coast open for explorers, trappers, hunters, miners, fur traders, adventurous settlers, Catholic missions down from the Canadian territory and the Protestant missions from the East Coast, the nagging conflict between the United States and the British-Canadians for control of the Northwestern territories, and the conflict in the Southwest with Mexico. The territories soon filled with United States forts and armies. These lands became *The Far West* in Woodard's listing of the nations, a territory that did not have much of a sense of its social unity, much less what it meant to be a state of the Union. Its contribution to the *American Character* was to heighten the individualistic features of Greater Appalachia and the Western Midlands as a conscious ideology of independence from state and federal governments, and develop the can-do of the rugged Westerner (cowboy; mountain man; etc.) who did not need to think of itself as belonging to the United States at all.

THE LEFT COAST

I have puzzled over Woodard's naming of the Pacific Coast as "left." Was it "left over" after the history of the expansion west? Or was it on the "left" side of the map when looking north? Or did it coyly indicate its difference from the East coast as "right." Woodard does not say or explain. But, getting ready for the sequel book on the American character which emphasizes the political conflicts between "individualism" (on the "right") and "communitarianism (on the "left"), Woodard describes the Pacific Coast as having a political mentality that is similar to that of New England (Yankeedom). And, he explains, it was settled by Easterners who sailed around the horn and entered the coastlands by sea, not by taking the Westward Ho trails overland. There on the coastlands the newcomers found that the Russian explorers, Spanish missions, and the culture of El Norte had already been there and left their mark upon the lands and its peoples. Since this earlier history was tolerant and open toward newcomers, and since the land was vast and not overrun by the earlier peoples, the coast was clear for the challenges of receiving new immigrants and becoming states of the United States. The major centers that mattered most were San Francisco and Los Angeles. In San Francisco the influence of the Eastern nations, especially Yankeedom and New York, was encouraged by those who had come to California, often by sea, from those states. Thus the often noted parallels between the California mentality and that of Yankeedom.

Nations and Races

THE AMERICAN CHARACTER

In *The American Character* Woodard retraces the history of the United States as the story of *The Eleven Nations* in their struggles to fit into the United States as a cultural and political unit. The main point is that there never was a *United* States in the sense of a society with a common culture. The United States was a legal structure created by the Constitution as a Federal Union under the duress of the Revolutionary War and the pressures put upon the several nations to agree together to oppose the British forces in the interest of financial and military independence. The major cultural differences among the nations came from their particular European extractions, as well as the various ways in which they made use of the lands they colonized in America, and especially the ideological positions they took during this period of creating the Federal Union. Their European histories and self-understandings were left in place and conflicts were answered by various compromises in order to form the legal entity soon to be called the "United States." This period of tussle was not resolved until the Civil War which was fought over the slavery issue, a war that did not resolve the slavery issue, but did determine that the South would be part of the Federal Union whether they liked it or not.

As Woodard rehearses this history of struggles among the eleven nations, he calls it "A History of the Epic Struggle Between Individual Liberty and the Common Good" (the subtitle). He emphasizes the way in which what we now call the concept of *Individualism* pervaded the American mentality throughout the many changes in our social and political histories. Individualism has never been conceptualized, questioned, or challenged by the several turns taken in our social histories in America. Its contrastive partner, that Woodard calls the *Common Good,* is also a largely unused term for the ideology he wants to emphasize as the vision of a "communitarian society." As with the concept of Individualism, the idea of the Common Good has never surfaced as a significant factor in the way political parties have formed ideologies or analysts have rendered their cultural critiques. But since Woodard sees that our malaise at the beginning of the twenty-first century is critical without a concept of what the United States stands for as a nation, he seeks to unearth the notion of the common good in its New England origins. It was fundamental to the Yankee view of society as a community interested in the well-being of all its citizens and of the United States as a nation committed to the Common Good. It was a vision of the Puritans taken from the Calvinistic tradition of Protestantism that had taken root in the New England states and inadvertently had given Yankeedom the intellectual leadership in much of the early history of Congresses and the writing of the Constitution of the United States. As an intellectual tradition it played a role in the debates that took place as the aristocratic "fathers" of the United States were at work on the Constitution. And as a cultural vision the idea of a communitarian society influenced the slightly later abolitionist movements in New England and the thinking of President Lincoln who was committed to the concept of the Union which then became a reason for his response to the secession of South Carolina and the decision to go to war (Civil War).

At every step in both the earlier and later histories, there was opposition from the Deep South that continued its preference for the slave state model, and its resentment against Yankeedom as the power behind the United States as a political and legal society. This interjected a third factor in the history of America's struggle to envision a "communitarian society," a factor that Woodard mentions but does not analyze. One might have thought that Woodard would analyze the Deep South in terms of his individualism-communitarian dialectic that has had such an effect upon the American character. Perhaps he realized that individualism was in some ways a character trait of Western civilization since its beginning, and that it was pervasive throughout all of the eleven nations and need not be analyzed in relation to the slave state Oligarchy of the South. But as a trait of American character, he pointed to its exaggeration in the traditions flowing from the clan-based individuals who populated the Midlands and Appalachia, those who resisted the constraints of "society" and "government." There was apparently no need to dwell on its appearance in the Deep South, even though it was there that the oligarchy's attitude toward slaves and the poor infiltrated the concept of individualism that became the fundamental mentality of Republicans after the Civil War and infected the conservative Protestantism when it became conscious of its political voice in the transition from Democrats to Republicans in the twentieth century. It would be helpful to know more about the way Individualism worked in the South in order to understand the thinking of the Republican "Southern Strategy," the emergence of the Tea Party Republicans, and the current Republican fixation on Individualism and anti-government commitments in alignment with their antipathy of social welfare.

Woodard's separation of character traits into the attitudes permeating the several "nations" could then be described in terms of their political histories. At the current stage of these histories, the ideologies of "Individual Liberty" become characteristic features of the Republicans, and the ideologies of the "Common Good" support the Democrats and their ideas of a "Communitarian Society" (welfare state). Woodard concludes this history and these studies with some statements about the issues between the "red" and the "blue" states that are unresolved and that frustrate the very idea of a *United* States. He then emphasizes that the political issue is rooted in our failure to find a way to create an economy that can serve both the values of individualism and that of a communitarian society. His answer is that a compromise is necessary at the political level, and that, now that the Deep South is Republican, the age-old tension between the Deep South and Yankeedom will have to redefine the political issue that has to be solved by the solution Woodard has in mind, namely to work for a political "compromise." This solution stays mainly at the level of the financial and political structures of the society.

My own sense of the issues that have erupted recently in Amerca is that they cannot be solved solely by means of a compromise in matters of the economy and financial institutions, whether such is possible at all under our current circumstances. Part of the problem is that the two political parties, the Republican and the Democratic, have allowed the financial and corporate institutions to have their way with the governance of the society. There is simply no regulation of financial institutions or global corporations. Thus the parties no longer have political leadership or power capable of addressing the issues that have occurred in the last century, or even of imagining a healthy and working society. The parties have not been able to see that the current president's myopic vision of a "great society" is not an answer to our malaise, but a very serious threat to the well-being of America, the global world of nations, and the planet earth. Neither Woodard nor Trump proposes any vision or set of policies to stop the unraveling of the society that was on the way to a consideration of the common good. Instead, we have a concentrated focus on a single issue politics (taxes/wealth) and a cadre of white male politicians' intent on ridding the nation of "other" cultures. This means that Woodard's depiction of American character, as helpful as it has been to focus on the characteristics of the "nations" instead of the "states," a focus that asks us to consider the economic reasons involved in the ideologies of the several nations, has not analyzed either the social configurations or the mentalities underlying the ideologies sufficiently to grasp the complexity of the current situation of crisis. We can certainly thank Woodard for a breathtaking breakthrough in making our collective histories available for serious discussion and revision. But if we want to join the Yale Professors in their quest for a principle of authority, not only in the twentieth century in Europe, but especially in the twenty- and twenty-first centuries in America, we have to make the social situation even more complex and ask about our multicultural configuration and the problem of mythic mentality that has not even been broached. In this chapter I want to introduce two other "nations" among us that need to be part of the picture as we consider our social and cultural crisis.

OTHER NATIONS AND OTHER CHARACTER TRAITS

There are several other peoples and cultures in America that should be added to Woodard's list of "nations" and the description of our current malaise. They include several immigrant ethnicities, the African Americans, the disenfranchised women now finally coming to speech and being heard, the impoverished poor as a class created by the Republicans' fixation on late capitalism, and the native Americans ("Indians"). From this list of "others" I have selected two for a brief description: our Native Americans and our African Americans, leaving the analysis of capitalism's influence on others until a later chapter. These two "nations" are of great significance for the American story that Woodard mentions but does not discuss in any detail and does not include in his list of "eleven nations." If we want to understand the history of the American "character," these two nations have to be in the picture. I want therefore to discuss briefly their significance.

The Indian Nations

Woodard mentions the native Americans who were encountered by the various American nations in the process of their settlements along the Eastern Sea Coast, and their early histories in the formation of the United States. But he stays at the level of the popular American story in which the Indians figure as the indigenous tribes that sometimes help the settlers, sometimes agree to "treaties" with the "White Man," sometimes find themselves resenting broken promises, thus needing to find ways to complain, and sometimes deciding to resist. Only in the Canadian territories did the European (French) settlers consider the resident native Americans their equals as those who already inhabited the land. The French treated them as citizens of the territory. The European immigrant-nations to their South were unable to consider any kind of equality with the Indians, treated them as an inferior race to be instructed in the White man's ways, and considered the lands upon which they were living as free for the taking and for colonization, not the property of the Indians. For the next two hundred years, even in those cases where the European immigrants and Federal government agents sought to write up treaties in order to guarantee "agreements" with the natives, a basically legal language defined the relationship (promises, agreements, laws, payments, threats, and punishments). Reading the statements made by American officials to the Indians and cited in documentary records, one is made aware of the naivite of the American mentality that assumed that the Indians would understand the contract language of a treaty. Beneath it all were the assumptions and practices of the Western capitalistic social system with its notions of property, ownership, contracts, and the assignment of values mainly in terms of money. As Richard Spencer, a leader of white nationalism, has said: "At the end of the day, America *belongs* to the white man... We *gave* the Indians lands for their reservations." He did not say how Americans came to own the lands. But the treaties, formulated exclusively by American agents who considered the lands the "property" of the United States, were written as business contracts. The treaties also spelled out the punishments for failure to comply with the agreements. Then, as the story of the "taking of the West" began to unroll, and the ill conceived "treaties" went awry, the American response to the natives' failure to live up to the terms of an agreement was invariably the use of the military to punish the Indians and force them to live on the "reservations" they had been "granted" as their "property." These reservations were considered by the Americans to be sufficient for the sustenance of the Indians if only they would settle down and learn to farm, work, and accommodate Western ways. The Indians were turned into a class of people living on "reservations," rejected as citizens integral to the American culture. And the "Indian Wars" in our history, which could be used to explore the instructive cultural issues that arose when we first met those who already lived here in this "new land," have never emphasized the cultural issues or our mistreatment of the Indians, only our victories over their resistance (Bull Run; Little Bighorn; Wounded Knee; Apache Wars).

Since Woodard does not emphasize or analyze this feature of our "character," I want to mention a book by Alvin M. Josephy, Jr. called *The Nez*

Critical Times for America

Perce Indians and the Opening of the Northwest (Yale University Press, 1971). This history runs to 667 pages in the "abridged edition" and is packed with thorough documentation of the encounters with these peace-loving natives of the northern Rockies. The history runs from the Lewis and Clark expedition (1805) in which they were "friendly" and offered help and guidance over the Rockies, through the seventy-five years of American aggressions of their lands (invasions; broken treaties and promises; miners and settlers simply moving in; and armies galore marching from California, Vancouver, Olympia, Colorado, and Keogh), to the final surrender of Chief Joseph and the several hundred Nez Perce Indians and their children, stock, and horses after a retreat of 1,700 miles from the Idaho territory on the Western side of the Rockies (the Wallowa Valley, Lapwai, where they had their home areas), through the Rockies to the East, and almost to the Canadian border (1877). As Josephy sums up this history of invasions by the White men (traders, miners, foresters, settlers, and militia after militia of volunteers, state and federal army personnel under their generals) he says:

> The Nez Perce, leaving Idaho with approximately 750 persons, including women, children, and sick and old people, with all their baggage and a huge horse herd, had conducted an unprecedented 1,700-mile retreat, fighting almost all the way. Altogether, the Indians had battled some two thousand regulars and volunteers of different military units, together with their Indian auxiliaries of many tribes, in a total of eighteen engagements including four major battles and at least four fiercely contested skirmishes. At least 120 of their people had been killed, including some sixty-five men and fifty-five women and children, and they had slain approximately 180 whites and wounded 150. Man for man, they had proven themselves better fighting men and marksmen than the soldiers ... The Nez Perce survivors of the struggle, once a rich and self-sufficient people, were made destitute ... The Indians had lost their horses, cattle, guns, personal possessions, savings of gold dust and cash, homes, freedom—everything but their honor.[1]

After the surrender the Nez Perce tribe came to be seen as a remarkable people of the Western lands, and Chief Joseph was invited to Washington. In his "surrender speech" he said:

> I know that my race must change. We cannot hold our own with the white men as we are. We only ask to be recognized as men. We ask that the same law shall work alike on all men ... Let me be a

---

1. Josephy, *Nez Perce Indians*, 612–13.

free man—free to travel, free to stop, free to work, free to trade, where I choose, free to choose my own teachers, free to follow the religion of my fathers, free to think and talk and act for myself— and I will obey every law, or submit to the penalty.[2]

Reading this history of what has been called the "Nez Perce war," and pondering the culture of our native Americans, that they were not inferior human beings at all, we can see that we Americans had not been able to appreciate their remarkable way of life because its own culture and mindset placed them outside the world in which we lived. Our assumptions about them were false, and our efforts to force them to assimilate our Western ways were misguided. For me, questions about cross cultural understanding came tumbling out, challenging the American mono-cultural mentality and what Woodard calls our "character." The striking contrast between the two cultures, and the inability of the Anglo-Americans to engage that of the native Americans as an authentic human cultivation, actually became an indictment of our own Western culture and its sense of superiority and righteousness in relations with other peoples. Our failure to engage the Native Americans was more than an "inability." It was an unwillingness, a mark of our character.

Since my son, Curtis Mack, had worked as the wildlife manager for the Nez Perce for forty years and was well acquainted with their tribal ways and people, I wondered whether I would be welcome to come and talk to the tribal council at Lapwai. This turned into an invitation from the Tribe to attend a Potlach in Lapwai for a family's celebration of a son's birthday. As the reader may know, the Potlach ritual among tribes in the Pacific Northwest is a way to celebrate personal and tribal events by reversing the patterns of exchange. In the case of an event celebrating the tribal chief, he may take all of the gifts that have been given to him as the chief in the course of a year and give them back to the people in the course of the ritual. In the case of the Potlach I experienced at Lapwai, the drums were beating and the people danced, the birthday youth leading the column for the first few times around. On occasion the drums would stop and the parents of the boy being celebrated would draw a ticket from a basket, select a gift from a large pile of boxes and utensils and give it to the person whose name was on the ticket. Many woolen Hudson's Bay blankets were among the gifts, as well as tribal rugs, mats and other useful items. And then the dancing would commence again. The dancing line grew longer and longer, and hundreds of

2. Josephy, *Nez Perce Indians*, 622.

gifts were distributed. Some of the younger men wore their American Army uniforms. All the people had costumes and the dancing continued into the night. My spouse and I also were invited to dance as guests of the tribe and family. We did not have to ask about the army uniforms. They marked the pride of these Nez Perce who had assimilated into the American society even while retaining what they could of their native American culture. To ask them to explain what to us must have been a profound transformation of cultural identity and attitude was hardly possible on such an occasion. It might not be possible on any occasion, striking as it would to the foundational logics of both cultures, and the need to let features of both relax long enough to take a turn on the dancing floor in order to see how it felt to dance to the drums and music of the other.

It has been two hundred years of racial injustice and national prejudice at the most physical level of social domination and rejection. And yet, these Nez Perce, in ways similar to many of the Native American tribes, found ways to respond to our aggression in remarkably humanizing ways. I would like to think that this brief sharing of a personal experience with them might illustrate the profound intercultural consequences of such cross-cultural tragedy, together with the clear possibility of real cross-cultural learning. It is time for the American sense of superiority, rooted as it is in the Western Christian traditions, to yield to the principle of equality and experience just how wonderful human relations in a multicultural world can be.

The African Americans

Since Trump, America's history of slavery and treatment of African Americans can be seen as a deeply embedded racial prejudice. We can now call it *white supremacy* and ask about its effects in our politics and self-understanding as a nation. In a recent publication by Ta-Nehisi Coates called *We Were Eight Years in Power* (One World, 2017), the effects of this racism is documented throughout our history and shown to be rooted in what Coates calls the "sin" of American society, namely the slavery of the African Americans that continues to affect all of our attitudes about social injustices and political programs. It is this social practice that, when noticed as a "sin" (Coates's knowing use of the Christian term with a smile that does not dismiss its radical intention), has always required denial. The denial has taken the many forms of rationalization as reasons and excuses for the practice that pervades our society and lets the practice and historic events stand as "natural," if not according to God's own view of the descendants of Ham as recorded in the Bible. The curious thing about this denial is that the rationalizations always occur at a second level of reflection and response, allowing the fact of racism to continue to reside in the mentality at a basic level of our social anthropology. Coates does not delve into this academic and theoretical issue, even though his understanding of the issue is clear, thorough, and radical. Instead, he tells the stories of himself as a "black" person growing up in America; the history of the African Americans in America by means of selected incidents; the history of typical responses on the part of American intellectuals and politicians; and a survey of the political history of the Obama presidency and the Trump administration. It is a brilliant book, consisting of essays written for the *Atlantic* now organized as an anthology around the theme of "notes" for the "eight years" of Obama's presidency as a black man. As Toni Morrison has written in her recommendation of the book: "I've been wondering who might fill the intellectual void that plagued me after James Baldwin died. Clearly it is Ta-Nehisi Coates."

Coates tells these stories as moments in the history they reveal. This history does not need documentation. Many of the incidents and citations are already somehow familiar. And Coates's theory of the "problem" underlying the history does not need argumentation. The "problem" has been the way Anglo Americans have taken the fact of African Americans among us as slaves for granted without finding it ugly and offensive. But the collection of these incidents and statements have details and historical context complete enough to count as a documentation that can no longer be swept aside. And interwoven, they create a stunning record of the "problem," not merely as a social issue that needs to be corrected as sometimes recognized, but as America's social-psychological disease. It is the ease with which African Americans have been used as slaves, and the difficulty that Americans have had to acknowledge the effects of this irreparable trafficking in human beings, that Coates diagnoses as a social and mental disease. All of the "reasons" that have been used to "explain" this sordid social practice and circumstance, from the Bible, theology, social Darwinism, cultural differences, cultural lag, mental incapacity, and criminal psyches, have been extreme rationalizations in the interest of covering up the fact of the Anglo Americans' reasons for engaging in the slave trade in the first place, and treating the slaves as inferior beings. It has been a horrendous and ugly history, and the rationalizations do not suffice to keep us from noting that. They are not explanations. They are denials.

Critical Times for America

This review need not rehearse the list of social injustices Coates handles, nor the political attempts at reparation that did not and cannot succeed. A mention of a few well known events is sufficient to make the point. There was the resurgence of lynching during and after Reconstruction without legal ramifications. There were the many attempts to keep African Americans from having the vote. There were the several thoughtless programs intended to address the impoverishment of the "blacks" as if slavery were their own fault. There was the deceitful use of "restricted covenants" and "financial contracts" to keep "blacks" out of white neighborhoods. There was the segregation of schools. And there was the vicious set of laws that insured the incarceration of African Americans at a degree much higher than that of others. The results of all of these ineffective social programs, from city zoning laws to the FHA, have to be seen as racist. And one of the remarkable features of the history Coates tells is that those in power who actually controlled the programs and blamed the "blacks" for their failures were apparently oblivious to their own deeply embedded racism. This feature occurs again and again in citations from leading politicians that rant against the few attempts America has made to remedy the social injustices against the African Americans. The result is a history that documents racism as essential to American attitudes about the "blacks," often entangled in political bills and propositions that can only be understood as rationalizations for perpetuating injustices. That slaves were commodities and slavery was basic to a primary economy has given the social psyche a fundamental attitude that has been very difficult to exhume. It is the refusal even to acknowledge that the practice of human predation on other humans is a very serious human disease.

After the eight years of Obama's administration, a phenomenon that brought out the best of latent Afro-American reflections upon a black presidency in white America, the shock of Trump's election reveals more. Coates does not make a special topic of the demonstration of white supremacy that has always been behind the racism in America as the ethnic mentality that has supported it. And it is not set forth by any of Trump's courtiers as the reasons for their political views. And yet, the fact of its influence has been noted by others time and again in the actions, proposals, and practices of his collection of courtiers. It is even there in the striking call for "nationalism" as a contrast to democracy that Steve Bannon has made, and that Trump has emboldened. Looking at the shock of his election in retrospect, it has become ever more clear that his success with the electorate as a show person celebrity was never convincing to thoughtful persons. His brash demeanor and empty promises were distractions from the real reasons for his hatreds of both Obama (a black!) and Hillary (a woman!). Both of these hatreds are anchored in the mentality of White (Male) Supremacy. Trump and his courtiers have not set themselves forth expressly as white supremacists, but their words and deeds certainly have betrayed them. And their fear of having a black president, or a woman president, is now obvious in the irrational ideological position of wanting to erase Obama's legacy on the one hand, and destroy the progressives' power and influence on the other.

CONCLUSION

Suppose we put these three histories of America together and compare our social situation with that of Europe in its *Quest for a Principle of Authority* (Chapter 1). What can we learn? The European quest took place in the void of social leadership that was created by the erosion of Christendom and the fragmentation of the petty kingdoms created by Protestantism. Then the histories of colonialism, global trading companies, and the Industrial Revolution took advantage of the void and aggravated the uncertainties about civil society and social instability. It was the time for intellectuals like John Stuart Mill, authors such as Charles Dickens, and cultural critics like Karl Marx to probe the question of a continuing influence of Western civility and Civilization. They were asking this question even as the peasants struggled for sustenance in the cities, having been dislodged from their feudal estates and societies. At the penultimate level of the kingdoms and nation-states there was a flurry of philosophical and political essays proposing social revisions of the petty kingdoms remaining. The French Revolution (1798–1815) had actually brought down the royal house of France but could not find a way to replace it. In the turmoil it was a military general (Napoleon) who rode forth on his horse to conquer much of Europe in the name of a new European unity of nations under his control. The subsequent period of military battles among the European nations, and the failure of its wars to solve the problems of unity, authority, and stable societies without a king, left the questions about national identity, governance, and purpose wide open. It was into this void that the rise of fascism took place as the final mark of the failure of Western Civilization to imagine and construct a stable, common good society without a monarch.

Critical Times for America

The fascists were solitary individuals who stepped forth without traditional credentials to pose as leaders of their nations. They claimed authority to rule in the name of their national histories which they evoked with modern slogans. These nations were marked primarily by racial ethnicity and common language: France, Germany, Spain, Italy, Russia, Prussia, Poland, Austria, and so forth. The leaders who stepped forth were very serious self-confident individuals who saw the troubled times as threats to their nation's destiny, and thought their situations called for buttressing the fractured structures and renewing the boundaries of the nations as they once were. Looking back, we can see that they were incapable of analyzing the political situations that had caused their discontent, and did not have a clear idea of what a nation (their nation) had to do in order to be a stable society that made well-being possible for all of their people. They nevertheless thought that their capacities as strong men were enough to force the changes, and that the availability of military force was enough to secure the necessary changes. In their efforts they became the images of authoritarian fascism, the embodiments of self-appointed power, those with the right to order ethnic cleansings, the instigators of racist nationalism, and the surfacing of a social psychological disease of Western civilization that has come to be called white male supremacy in the United States.

In the United States there was no political void of the European kind (many warring kingdoms without pope, God, or emperor) to explain the rise of the Tea Party Republicans and Donald Trump. Our culture critics are even now trying to assess the malaise among the people that the financial policies of the Republicans and Neoliberals created in their march from Reagan to the Bushes. But since this phase of our fall into social injustices and economic inequality is so complex in its influence and workings, the experts are having a difficult time explaining the current situation to the people. We have, however, learned that wealth inequality is the sign of capitalism's rule as the real power of our secular society. And we were becoming accustomed to trying to make sense out of the fantasies of virtual reality as the media learned to report the social news and entertainment. But we were not ready for the strut of a wealthy showman crossing the stage of a presidential campaign with nothing to offer except slogans of Making America Great Again. Our poor electorate. Accustomed to TV, social media, and Fox News, they were not prepared to see that Trump was incapable of the leadership we needed. He was not even capable of caring about the social issues facing the nation, much less providing leadership for America in a twenty-first-century global world of nations. But for those concerned about the social issues and the celebrity president, the first signs of a fascist psyche were obvious in his personality and behavior. That should have been enough to reject his candidacy. But his disparagement of the legacy of the Democrats, and especially that of a black president and woman candidate (precisely and only because the one was black, and the other a woman), were already creating enough political furor to cancel out deliberation. And so the electorate was offered a charismatic display of impulse and anger instead of the customary list of policies and promises. And the electorate was not able to tell the difference.

Thus the social situation that Trump and his Republican cohorts railed against is not similar to the European situation that eventuated in fascism's horrors. Ours is truly a post-Republican economic malaise created by the Republicans themselves. They blame it on the Democrats, of course, but have no appreciation for or concept of the social order the Democrats had been working on for more than one hundred years. That is the feature of the disparagement by the Republicans that is so disheartening and serious. Democrats were thinking that our legacy of concern for social justice, reasonable wages, welfare agencies, egalitarian morals, and a stable society aimed at the well-being of all citizens surely must be appreciated as a reasonable attempt to create a society worth living in, worthy of the tradition of Western civilization in the new context of a multicultural global world. What a surprise to learn that, according to Steve Bannon the Republicans want to smash this legacy into oblivion, and that the fundamental principle of governance was now to be "economic nationalism," a ridiculous statement of adolescent me-ism, a projection of personal desire as if it could be a policy for a whole world in which to live. Capitalism has won, it seems, at least in the world of the Trump administration. Trump and his cohorts have made it plain that the only things that matter (to them) are money, greatness, sovereignty, and (must we not admit it?) white supremacy. The use of force similar to the European fascists has not (yet?) exploded into violence. But there is the possibility of nuclear war at the level of global diplomacy and the constant use of threat, intimidation, and the police at the social and political levels here at home. With the appointments of incompetent loyalists to the president's cabinet and agencies, those who have been the critics of the very agencies and purposes to which they are now in charge, the dismantling of the Democratic vision of a safe, solid, and sane society is surely underway. The Democrats have repeatedly asked their Republican counterparts to spell out the vision of the society toward which their policies are aimed. But they have not done that, given the fact that they do not seem to have such a vision in the first place. They may not have any vision at all, actually, mesmerized with the money game as they all are, and thinking only about what the next move calls for in their own interests. Capitalism has won, not only as the power that drives the Republican political machine, but as the atmosphere and culture driving society and its mentality as well. America, it seems, has lost its memory of its history, of the way the nation once thought of itself and functioned.

So Woodard is right to retell our story and remind us of the fundamental conflict underlying the Republican-Democratic tension as a conflict between Individualism and Communitarianism. These are ideologies that are now in a locked stalemate over economic policy, as if finances are all that matters. And the comparison of Woodard's history of the American Nations with the European Quest for a Principle of Authority, when focused on the Individual with power who is incapable of imagining the welfare of society as that which is at stake, is most instructive. Who would have thought that the history of Western Civilization and its sciences was clever enough to produce an American society big enough, wealthy enough, and strong enough to bring the entire world of nations and their planet earth to the brink of destruction? The radical individualism of a Tea Party mentality with a psychotic president whose mental incapacity and impulsive behavior are enamored with the destruction of critics does not paint a pretty picture of the leader of the human race standing on the edge of the cliff waiting for the countdown. If we had developed a *cabaret* on the European model you could almost hear the banter on the edge of the abyss: "Leave the money when you jump!" To use the title of Noam Chomsky's book, *Optimism Over Despair*, and to follow his arguments throughout his thorough analysis of the despairing circumstances of our situation, only to admit that he cannot really say what the reasons are for hope, I would say that we American progressives can at least be thankful for the bumps in Trump's road. He may be as ego-centric as the European fascists were as individuals, and perhaps quite a bit more impulsive in his adolescence, but there are bumps in the American road that may have a chance to slow him down if not stop him before it is too late. What are the bumps? The media, the courts, the people in the Pentagon that are still sane, the political structure of the federal United States that still has enough sense and energy to tell Trump No. And the electorate is showing signs of awareness in the direction of forming both political and non-political movements addressed to issues of social injustices and inequality. Both the women as a class and the blacks as a people are finding their voice. And there are regions, such as in California, where social intelligence and savvy have not been squashed by an incompetent federal president.

There is, of course, the rather dismal mood in the United States in general, and what our social analysts are saying about the new age of social media/virtual reality, and the focus on entertainment in TV, newspapers, and theatre. These are observations of what might be called the popular culture that no longer reads books and newspapers. This culture is certainly part of our problem, if we want to consider our critical times and think about the future. In the next chapter I want to discuss this issue that Clive James calls "Cultural Amnesia." It will be a way to continue the study of our European precursors and ask about the importance of Western culture as it has been. It will also help clarify the price that is paid for consciously disparaging it (turning our back upon it, from Reagan on), consigning it to the faulty past (as in Postmodernism), and "forgetting it" (as in the "cultural amnesia" of the burgeoning social media). It is not only Trump's personal psychology that sooner or later needs to be addressed. It is the failure of American mentality to recognize and address the mythology of the Western Christian tradition at the core of our inability to live in a multicultural world. Cultures do not easily disappear. And they are not eagerly taken up for critical analysis. But it may be that the time has come to create a conversation about our nation as an heir of the Western tradition facing a most uncertain future.

3

Cultural Amnesia
Intellectual Voices in the Wilderness

So far we have had the human enterprise of social formation in view as a political entity. This has allowed us to ask about the "quest for a principle of authority" in last-century Europe, national leaders as strong men, the emergence and failures of fascism, race as a marker of nationalism, the character of the American nations, and the conflict of economic ideologies as in need of compromise. If we want to think about a society that does not need exploitation, war, and violence, however, we need to recognize that the concept of *culture* has not been addressed. It is culture that provides the symbols of significance for a society as a social formation with a meaningful history, as well as the grammar for thinking about its social issues and the logic of its social ethos. Cultural logics can also be used to rationalize conquest and violence, of course. So we need to spend some time making sure we understand the way our culture works. Western culture has been rooted in the myths and rituals basic for Christendom, on the one hand, and the development of what we have come to call the *humanities*, on the other. The role of Christendom in the tradition and history of Western civilization has always been more or less clear as the religious institution of Catholicism even if not thought about as a grammar for its social formations the size of its empires. And the role of the humanities has been even more conscious and clear at the level of intellectuals and the academy, but now seems to be in decline itself. The humanities stem from the Renaissance and Enlightenment periods of self-consciousness as intellectual beings. The result of these awakenings was the awareness of the beauty of the natural order; the awareness of being an individual person; the awareness of the collective as a society; the awareness of *history* as the past of one's society; *literature* as the archive and documentation for history; *philosophy* as the analysis of a society's myths, history, and meanings (symbols); *science*; the emergence of the academy (discourse, conversation among intellectuals, classrooms and forums for discussion); and intellectual traditions about the meaning of individual and social existence studied by scholars, but available to all in books, media, and institutions of religion, education, and research. Much of that history is distinctive of Western civilization.

The arts and sciences, as well as most intellectual traditions of the humanities, were alive and well in the histories of the American academies until the 1960s of the last century. That was when America's sense of leadership, superiority, and a brief period of supremacy in the world of nations ran into trouble in Viet Nam. Students began to question our interventions in other nations, and especially our use of the military to "spread democracy." It was also the time when the abuse of African Americans became a noteworthy and unresolved social issue. There was unrest about courses that, in the eyes of the students, were not relevant to the social issues of the times. They wanted to learn about African American culture, native American Indians, and why Americans could not treat all cultures the same. There was something about Western and American culture that gave these students the sense that something had gone wrong, that our society should not be working the way it was. The Harvard faculty met to respond to this unrest and created what they called the "core curriculum" in English and Literature. This core curriculum was essentially a set of the traditional courses in (Western) philosophy, history and literature. Students were not impressed. They wanted to ask about democracy, war, global politics and the ethics of governmental social behavior in the treatment of Native Americans, African Americans, and immigrants from Asian and Near Eastern countries. They wanted to read the authors of "other" cultures such as Borges, Baldwin, and Malcom X. Culture critics began to talk about a shift in cultural mentality at the level of the populous. Television and talk show media were the way information was being shared. Television turned to entertainment and eventually to the non-literary world of smart phones, social media, and fake news. Some cultural critics, such as David Harvey and Fredric Jameson, noticed that reading books was no longer the way the populous was being informed. They put this together with the academics in literature who were talking about Postmodernism and the "end" of the Western narrative of civilization that once had been the source for the intellectuals' categories of culture and society. Essays were written about the rapid-fire stimuli of images that made it difficult if not impossible to deliberate and think clearly about the social world. I had to discuss this period of cultural critique in the *Rise and Fall* book (Yale) as one of the reasons for the erosion of the "big picture" projected by the Christian myth and its cultural grammar, the project upon which I had been working for the past several years.

When a colleague at a university in the East read my Yale book (*The Rise and Fall of the Christian Myth*), and understood it as my departure from working in "Christian Origins" as a biblical scholar, he sent me a copy of *Cultural Amnesia* by Clive James (Norton, 2007) without a word of explanation. I said to myself "What's this?" But Marcel Mauss had made it clear that to question a gift was tantamount to its rejection, so I decided to have a look. It is a large and very heavy tome of 876 pages by an author with whom I was not acquainted. It was not a monograph or a single essay, but a collection of mini essays on 106 authors and artists whom James had read during his career, also as an author, producer and art critic. Throughout he had taken notes on his readings, conversations, and reflections. He was obviously skilled in the analysis of style, content, and the personal histories of these authors, and had decided to sum up his career of readings with this volume of mini essays about what these authors had written. What a feast of intellectual servings. Most were well known European figures, also many Americans, and most from the nineteenth and twentieth centuries. He himself, an Australian, had a deeply held commitment to and love for the *humanities*, as he says, that apparently had given him the energy to pursue these authors and their books in his travels. Sometimes he was in Sydney, or London, Germany, Paris, or New York, to work on his own writings or shows, but also to track down another author and ask the questions their writings raised for him. It was the significance of the Western tradition of the arts and literature that drove his quest. He would tell of his coming across a rare book in an antiquities store by an author not well known, buy it and repair to a café to sit down and read it. He would invariably take notes, sometimes marking the margins of the books if need be. It was clear that these authors and their writings constituted a level of society within which James lived as his cultural world.

Cultural Amnesia

I was curious about the terms in the title, *Culture* and *Amnesia*, and wanted to know how James defined each of them. But he did not provide definitions. Nowhere did he develop a theory of culture, nor an explanation of his own reasons for the enticement culture had for him, nor why the topic of *amnesia* was needed. The answers to these questions had to be found in the reading of the mini essays on the 106 figures. I noticed that it was a roster of writers, of course, but not all of them were recognized as literary artists. And while the mini essays described the writings and commented upon matters of style and cultural insight, they also included James's observations of an author's readings of still other authors. There were conflicts of ideology that had to be mentioned, ways of subtle revision by one author of another's assumptions, and the avoidance at times of common topics that might have called for debate. All had written about the world in which they lived. And they all wanted to be read and understood in terms of the intentions one had for writing in the first place. It was a roster of social and culture critics at a very high level of literary skills. And James's selection spread out to include figures of historical importance for other reasons, such as Hitler, Tacitus, Ernesto Sabato, Norman Mailer, and Margaret Thatcher. Thus the set of descriptions reveals the way in which James traced the human figures of his own social-historical world and pondered the way each author thought about his/her own culture and society. There were also some personality conflicts to notice and explain, but most observations were in the interest of what might be called James's own standard of the *truth* of the literature that he registered in terms of what it had said about the culture it addressed. Oh my. It was a portrayal of a writer at work on understanding other writers, all in the interest of what James called *humanism*. It was humanity at work on the humanities. And it told me that James understood the function and importance of the academy's institution of forums and classrooms for the creation and sustenance of culture. James saw these scholars belonging to a class of scholars talking to one another via writings without the benefit of the classroom. They belonged to a discipline and its culture by means of their intellectual readings of one another and their projects of making sense to themselves. It was a veritable social psychology of dislodged academicians. It put me in my place as a would-be critic of the Western tradition who had thought to focus mainly on the Christian myth without having a roster of colleagues in the many disciplines such as these with whom to struggle. But reading James did not tell me I was wrong. That's because there was more.

Critical Times for America

I found myself putting James in his place as well. His frequent use of the terms *humanism* and *humanities* were at first problematic for me. I remember when the term *human* fell out of scholarly parlance as undefinable, a subtle glorification of "man" as a special kind of creature, if not the counterpart to the theological language of the divine/*human* drama. But as I moved to the studies of anthropology and ethnography in order to analyze religion and the human enterprise of social formation, the distinctive marks of our species became very significant in other ways. The human as a particular kind of species cannot be understood without an analysis of the capacity for language, abstract reasoning, and the influence of others ("family" and "tribe"). So here was James upping the ante on the distinctive features of the human species by focusing on its capacity for language and *writing*. He was doing this by reading writers who were reading writers and writing about culture. That James understood what he was doing by calling it an investigation of culture, and that the culture he was investigating was rooted in *humanism*, and that humanism was not simply a philosophic concept to hold a place for the troubled Western civilization, but a proper name for the activity that made our species what it was, told me that he understood the intellectual features of culture and society. And here I was reading James as a writer as he was reading other writers who were reading yet other writers, all with James's subtle reminder that it was all in order to avoid *amnesia*!

James's introductory essay about Vienna as the city of cafes, and the place where literary intellectuals of the nineteenth century pursued their culture, is absolutely precious. It sets the stage, however, for a recurring theme throughout the book. It is that many of these intellectuals were Jewish and the time was coming when Hitler would "put out the lights." Thus it was that the Nazis created a social situation throughout Europe that forced intellectuals to decide what to think and do about society. Many were deeply torn about their loyalty to a certain nation and culture even as it was being overrun by the Nazi military. James uses the figure of Sartre to observe this issue. Sartre stayed in Paris even after the Nazis had arrived, ducking into a small group of dissidents that should have become active protesters, according to James, but were not. Only after the war and the Nazis were gone did Sartre claim that he had not been pro-Nazi, that he had not cooperated with them. James considered this to have been dishonest, a lie that revealed a character flaw, and he makes this kind of soft reproof of others quite often in other mini essays. This told me that, for James, the humanities were not avocational to life as a social being, but fundamental. Reading and writing about society had to be honest, because society had an *ethos* that required its characters to have an *ethic*. The arts were not merely entertaining.

James assesses the character of all the writers in his list, always putting their writings on their social situations into some relation to that situation. *Character* was the term he used to assess that relationship. For James, one had to stay true to what one wrote (said) in order to be a respectable social and human being. Reading and writing in the humanities were the way in which one learned culture, expressed one's humanity, and contributed to its sustenance. Character was the result of taking culture seriously and making sure one's actions were in keeping with its *ethos*, or honest and pointed in their disagreement with it. Many artists and writers passed this test, and the book can easily be read as a celebration of the arts and sciences of Western civilization. There are profound and wonderful mini essays on Albert Camus, Alfred Einstein, Duke Ellington, Federico Fellini, Witold Gombrowicz, Franz Kafka, Thomas Mann, Montesquieu, Alfred Polgar, and others. All were seen by James as living under the threat of their culture coming to its end. One of James's heroes is Egon Friedell, an intellectual in Vienna in the late 1930s who was also a cabaret star. His *Kulturgeschichte der Neuzeit* was a publishing disaster in Germany because of the times (late 1920s?), and the German edition vanished, only a few copies to be found now in rare book stores. But it was translated into English in 1930 in London as *Cultural History of the Modern Age* (Paidoon) and then reprinted in German after the war and became a very successful publication in Germany as well because, as James says, "they needed him." Those who fled Germany after the war took copies of Friedell in German with them, because, as James says, "His writings give the comforting illusion that the historical accumulation of knowledge makes some kind of steadily increasing, and therefore irreversible sense." Unfortunately this sense was wiped out for Friedell himself when the *Anschluss* took place and he saw the Nazis coming for him out of his second story window. He jumped out, waving a warning to those below.

This *Anschluss*, suicide, and loss of Friedell's *Kulturgeschichte* gives us an indication of James's use of *amnesia*. We use this term for "memory loss," but Funk and Wagnalls defines it as "Partial or total loss or impairment of memory, involving restricted or extensive areas of experience." It is taken from psychiatry and thus has the connotation of having been caused by a shock or illness of some kind. James does not elaborate, but the descriptions of the social situations and circumstances confronted by his authors at work in the composition and evolution of social and cultural history tell us that the *amnesia* he had in mind is not simply a memory loss. It is a loss of the society and its culture humans create that make living worthwhile. He also knows that culture is the product of human thinking, and that it can be erased by the unthinking violence of a fascist leader. In America the *amnesia* of our cultural sensibility and history has been building since Reagan, but has been exacerbated by the shock of the election of an uncultured showman by an unthinking electorate to the presidency of the United States. Our media historians have been trying to figure out how that could have happened. And the observations they have come up with about the faults of our government, political parties, social histories, and social circumstances are certainly correct, but also most unenlightening. The main reason we are having trouble understanding this more or less recent set of events is that our observations and discussions stay at the popular level of social experience, consciousness, and public events while the cultural reasons for the chaos have not yet been analyzed or even recognized.

In the case of James's use of the humanities to pursue "culture" and think about the history of twentieth-century Europe, the culture he prized was that of classical humanisim anchored in the Greek roots of Western philosophy. But the social history of Europe had been changing, especially since the Reformation and the Industrial Revolution. The culture of James's humanism was still being pursued in the circles of writers and artists who functioned as elites in their societies. But they and their discourse, philosophy, and literary arts were finally no longer able to celebrate their social histories without being noticed as disruptive dissidents or critics of the fascist authorities and rulers. James was caught in an impossible pursuit of culture as if it were still meaningful for his societies as they had developed. His work is a clear example of the relation between culture and society, and the destructive effects possible when they conflict, when the mentalities of each no longer have the same logics. In this case the power in the hands of a strong man in charge of his society had developed a logic that was destructive of its erstwhile culture.

In the case of the recent American history, the mythic logic of Western civilization was in the process of being replaced by the secular logics of science and capitalism, neither of which had the culture in mind. James seems to have understood this failure of the Western culture he called humanism, but he apparently was not able to discuss it. He did, however, come to speech on the fact that literary artists who as intellectuals developed social *theories* and *ideologies* (ways of thinking about culture and society as philosophical concepts) were threats to the tradition of humanism as James understood it. His commitment was to a world of literary skill, intellectual exchange, and enjoyment rooted in the past when it had enhanced its social contexts and was appreciated even by the more materialistic interests of other social factions. The nineteenth and twentieth centuries no longer rewarded this world of the humanities and became divorced from the secular realm. There were many occasions in James when he found it necessary to say that an artist or literary critic should not be taken seriously as one worthy to be on his list of humanists because he/she made universalizing statements about some cultural-philosophical concept that did not fit with James's own view of humanism as an intellectual order that should not exist in separation from society and its political functions. Such an artist might be appreciated for his/her insights into human existence and skill in the way with words. But a reference to the traditional world of theory and philosophy that intended to be taken as meaningful in the present set of social circumstances interferred with James's appreciation of the artist for other reasons, namely for the artistic skills displayed in the observation of personal and human relational existence under social stress, a skill that James thought profound. This was an astonishing thing to hear from a major proponent of the humanities. It meant that he somehow knew that the world of art and literature to which he had given his life existed now only in a separate mental compartment at a distance from both the social world he would have liked to live in, and from the philosophical rationales that should still have given society its reasons for its existence, but could not after the rise of fascism. No wonder those intellectuals who were concerned about the emergence of fascism in the modern period were not included on his list of authors worthy of reading. But they may, actually, not have had much to say about Hitler, Mussolini, and Stalin that could tell an artist what to say and how it was still possible to live in a world whose cultural tradition was coming to its end.

In America it has been the lack of insight into the thinking of Trump, if there is any cogent thinking to be found there, and that of the spokespersons for the policy makers in both the Republican and Democratic parties, that frustrates enlightened deliberation about our social situation. Our academic intellectuals should still be able to have something to say about the situation by noticing the gaps between the policies of this administration and the vision of the multicultural society we were in the process of constructing. But they are not saying much except that the Western tradition of culture is no longer clearly in evidence in our modern society and world. That is because the cultural rationale of the Western tradition, namely Greek philosophy and the Christian myth, that has provided the narrative logic for Western civilization is no longer articulated as a logic or rationale for policies and programs, and, in any case, has never been analyzed even by biblical scholars as the grammar for the mentality of modern Christians and its effect on modern society. Thus the question of the way we think as a people and culture is not a topic to be raised for discussion. It is actually no longer a topic at all. There is no awareness of the deeply seated cultural logics of our society to discuss. We do know that religions have myths and that myths can have narratives and logics. And we do know that other cultures have other religions, and that there is some connection between a religion and the mentality of another people. But these phenomena are never talked about as of significance for making an effective difference for the way our society works and responds to new situations. In the case of our consternation about the newly formed Trump administration, a situation that has shocked the other half of the populous, we not only do not know what to do, we do not know what to think or make of the situation.

We could read the recent book by Noam Chomsky on *Optimism over Despair* (Haymarket, 2017), a scholar and intellectual of our social history, directly addressing the problem of what to think and do about the situation, if we were still reading books. The subtitle, *On Capitalism, Empire, and Social Change*, announces a fascinating and thorough review of our social and political history as a preparation for describing the shocking Trump election and program as an unexpected and extremely dangerous political event that threatens the future of America, the world of nations, and the planet. So consternation is certainly called for. But one would have expected that Chomsky, our social historian and conscience, might tell us what to make of it and what we might do to improve the situation and our democracy. At the end of this excruciatingly clear description of the problem, C. J. Polychroniou, his interviewer, asks Chomsky about his statement that: "There are two grim shadows that loom over everything that we consider: environmental catastrophe and nuclear war . . ." before going on to ask: "Are you overall optimistic about the future of humanity, given the kind of creatures we are?" Chomsky's response is that: "We have two choices. We can be pessimistic, give up, and help ensure that the worst will happen. Or we can be optimistic, grasp the opportunities that surely exist, and maybe help make the world a better place. Not much of a choice."[1]

Given the title of the book, this was a disappointing conclusion. After his life of scholarly analysis of capitalism and politics, and his summary in this book of the crises now looming for the future of civilization because of the Trump campaign and election, Chomsky's answer drops down to the level of the personal choices we have, one of which is to "grasp the opportunities that surely exist, and maybe help make the world a better place." Throughout the book these "opportunities" are put forth in terms of grassroots efforts and voluntary organizations on the fringes of the current composition of society. The grassroots level is where persons might become involved with local issues about schools, join discussion groups about local politics, promote unions, form protest groups, etc. It may be that that is all we have as an opportunity to do something about our social ills, supposing the issue is clear enough and clearly in the interest of the well-being of the society as a whole. And it may also be that a further analysis of the ills of the society will not tell us any more about these ills to guide us in making our personal choices to correct them. Chomsky does suggest that he personally would like to see a new political party evolve, building on Sanders's campaign to upset the current lock down in Washington by the Tea Party Republicans. That is surely something to consider, even though an individual at the local level may not have much clout to help make it happen. Unfortunately, Chomsky does not think such an evolution probable. So we are left without much advice as to how to overcome the despair that has been developing, not because the grassroots have been doing the wrong things, but became the political system is obsessed with Republican power, wealth, and authority.

After reading Chomsky and after reading James we can see that the gap between "culture" and "society" has not been addressed by either intellectual. If culture is the arena of histories, symbols, and social logics (i.e. requires thinking); and if society is the arena of policies, actions, and social constructions (i.e. requires actions); the overlap has to be assessed before deciding what to do, whether a situation calls for celebration or for change. This means that the arena of culture is a very important component of a society as a social formation. In chapter 1 we ran up against the limits of traditional Western culture to propose a new political authority for Europe after the breakdown of Christendom and the Protestant kingdoms facing the

---

1. Chomsky and Polychroniou, *Optimism over Despair*, 196.

political uncertainties of the nineteenth and twentieth century and the need to ward off the rise of fascism. In chapter 2 we discovered that Woodard's history of America revealed the unyielding loyalty to the several cultural "origins" of the eleven nations, and that the conflicts among these cultures had not been overcome. According to Woodard there would have to be a political compromise at the level of financial policies. In this chapter, we see that Clive James looked for the "character" of his artists and authors in the humanities despite the threat of its ending in *amnesia*. And Chomsky's call to "make America better" is based on a thoroughly secular vision of our society without a consideration of what would be needed to make it better except to hope for a "new political movement." This means that *culture* is the problem, both for the analysis and understanding of the social and political issues of our time, and for imagining a vision of the future. We simply do not know what to make of our political situation, or what to do about it. Understanding the cultural mentality involved is a first step. It may not tell us what to do about the political influence this mentality is now having that needs to be addressed, but understanding its logic and cultural effectiveness can help us assess the reasons for our problematic situation.

There are actually two main mythologies in the Western cultural tradition that have been merged in our history and mentality. James was working with what we have called the "classical tradition," and this tradition, also called "the humanities", is clearly the most articulate and conscious cultural tradition among us. It harks back to the Greco-Roman era of Western civilization and has been cultivated primarily by the academic disciplines in literature and the arts, creating a class of elites whose voice, unfortunately, is seldom heard in the forums of politics. The other mythology within our Western tradition is that which is basic for Christianity, a biblical mythology clearly at work in the seminaries and treated as a "theology." A biblical mentality has been at work all along in Christianity as a "religion." James seems to have known about it, but avoided it as not part of the humanities. And Chomsky refers to it only at the level of religion as a social institution to characterize political ideologies. So Chomsky also has not addressed the mythic logic of the mentality involved. That is another reason for being disappointed in his recent publications. The narrative logic of the Christian myth is still informing the mentality America continues to use, although unconsciously. It needs to be surfaced for analysis.

I want therefore to refer to my own work on the narrative logic of the Christian myth. I had wanted to investigate that social logic in order to answer some questions about Christian origins in which a Society of Biblical Literature seminar of biblical scholars to which I belonged had been working. These questions indicated that I needed to consult with the ethnographers of tribal societies on their social theory of religion. The results of that research are available in several recent publications to be noted in the Bibliography. Then, when the September 11 event occurred and George W. Bush called upon the Bible to justify America's response as a declaration of war, I was startled and decided to write the book *Myth and the Christian Nation* (Equinox, 2008) in which I described the social logic of the myth. In a sequel publication, *Christian Mentality: The Entanglements of Power, Violence, and Fear* (Equinox, 2011), I applied the logic of the Christian myth to the social issues of America as they were evident during the twentieth century. I was eager to understand the effective difference the Christian myth made for the Western societies within which it had its place. One of the main findings of my studies was that the familiar narrative that starts with "Genesis," focuses on the Gospels, and ends with the "Revelation to John" (or the Apocalypse), provided a "historical" drama both for individuals and societies. For individuals, the Bible was the means to take Jesus seriously as the "Christ" and/or "personal savior" with a double vision of salvation or threat of judgment. For the church and its societies, the Bible was the narrative for seeing Western history as the divine plan for Christian missions with a double vision of a global kingdom of god or a destructive apocalypse at the end. Its power for Christians was the offer of a personal salvation and a secure place in the history of Christendom. Its logic applied to non-Christians, however, was that their place outside of Christendom called for divine judgment and destruction, creating the need to convert and become Christians. Since this double logic (of the singular and the dual) has driven the Christian and American missions to tell the rest of humanity and the world what they need to do to be "accepted" as persons and societies, it is the logic of this view of the world that has become dangerous and should be toned down, if not thoroughly revised. That has not happened because the Christian myth has settled into the imagination of the society at the level of the collective unconscious, as all myths do, and continues to work as a kind of mythic mind-set that tells us about the way the world works.

Historians and culture critics had been talking about the fading of Christianity as a mentality and religion, of course, pointing to such things as the shifts in membership away from traditional denominations to the independent and mega churches, the fragmentation of Catholic Christendom and the plurification of the Protestant varieties, as well as the way in which our government and state agencies now operate on the basis of self-interest and political policies instead of religious faiths. All of this is certainly true. But when the Bush II administration picked up on the notion of a "Christian Nation" after the 9/11 attack on the twin towers, and then used the term as a reference to our character as "righteous," and as an argument for going to war in response to the attack, and for our missions abroad, including our military invasions into the nations of the middle east, it became clear that the culture historians had been wrong about the fading of Christianity. Only certain social features and manifestations of Christianity had faded. These were the obvious characteristics of importance for churches as social institutions, such as their membership numbers. But numbers were not the only register of the pervasive mentality that remained. In Washington, at least, the *Christian Nation* was more than alive and well. It was clearly being used as an effective argument and self-understanding for the official response to the "attack." The languages of "evil," "righteousness," and "mission," taken from the vocabulary of Christianity, became clichés and rationales for a set of self-serving reasons for our "war on terror" and "missions" (read invasions) into the many nations of the Near East and throughout the world. Encouragement from the narrative logic of the Christian myth in politics, apart from the way the Bible had worked for individual congregations, was working as a national mythology. There were "saints" and "sinners" in the world of nations as political entities now, missions to instruct them in the American (Christian) way, and fascination with the righteousness of absolute power. Underneath it all was the threat of destruction if the "other" nations did not listen and conform. That also had a basis in the biblical story of God's plan. I thought it a strange violation of the customary separation of church and state, as well as of the distinction between religion and politics in most American Protestant traditions. The church was no longer the only social institution where "religion" was to be practiced. The state could also be an institution of "religion."

Then it occurred to me that others had also been troubled by not understanding the Christian features in Bush's politics of righteousness. One of these was Jeff Sharlet who wrote *The Family: The Secret Fundamentalism at the Heart of American Power* (HarperCollins, 2008), a thorough and upsetting investigation of an organization close to the White House that promoted and trained politicians in ultra conservative political thinking and strategy. And just as is the case with Trump and his coterie, there were frequent references to Hitler, Carl Schmitt, and the need for a single authoritarian leader. (See my *Rise and Fall*, 168, on American intellectuals involved in the ideology of "a super national sovereignty of intellectuals and bankers," and the notion of the "moral and natural right of these bankers and politicians to govern nations," as well as the "plan" to inaugurate the "New American Century," and more.) So I had to buckle down to yet another study of politics and religion, this time to assess what was going on in the Republican party's thinking about Christianity. What I had to discover was the way Republicans had put Christianity and power politics together, and why. That combination was not the customary way for Protestant Christians to think about Christianity and society.

Colin Woodard has been helpful in his description of Yankeedom as a colony of Puritans who were trained in the reformed Christianity of John Calvin. Calvin was a major Protestant Reformer of the sixteenth century who had settled in Geneva, Switzerland, where he created a theocratic society according to the teachings of Jesus and the Bible. It was highly moralistic and required absolute obedience to God's plan (*Institutes of the Christian Religion*). Calvin's influence in England included the Presbyterians and the Puritans, both of whom were Reformation reactions to the troubles England was having with the royal family and Catholicism. The Puritans came to Yankeeland from England and the Netherlands as families and built villages on the Genevan model. There would be central parks, churches, cemeteries, and civic buildings surrounded by plots of land sufficient to support a family. Families had to farm their plots, of course, but they were not all farmers. They were composed of craftsmen, shop owners, writers, civic leaders, lawyers, doctors, and teachers as well. Woodard spells this out as the setting for the social program and culture of Yankeedom with its town meetings, city councils, schools, and churches, as well as for the cultivation of its adamant hostility to the royal and aristocratic cultures of England and the Tidewater (*The Eleven Nations*, Chapter 3).

It was Yankeedom that influenced the American systems of universities, public education, egalitarian political philosophies, and attitudes against authoritarianism. It also gave us the original Republican political party. Yankeedom was conservative in the sense that it wanted its open society protected from changes that might threaten its values, with every person a citizen, and all working well in the pursuit of subsistence, education, culture, and well-being. Its intelligent and vibrant culture has lasted for over three hundred years, providing the nation with leaders, guidance, education, and political programs. But the years have taken their toll as the history of the United States unfolded. The Calvinism from the time of the Puritans formed networks of independent churches called Congregational, Presbyterian, and Baptist that branched out into other states and lands. Each continued to cultivate the concept of a moral society, but allowed Woodard's "communitarian" vision to accommodate the shape of the various nations of the United States. Then there was the emergence of the two party system, and the influence of the South as a very strong block of democratic interests in opposition to Yankeedom. As the Civil War and Reconstruction played out, it was the Republican Party that found a new base in the South where, apparently, it assimilated the Southern modifications on several cultural concepts. The notion of "freedom" now meant to be free from U.S. governmental control. The concept of the state was now that of a two-layered society (white and black). America as a country (land) was now to be the "property" of the owner of the "estate" (i.e., plantation), a single individual with the right and power to manage the finances and the workers (slaves). The "united" states became an oligarchy of states with "states' rights." And the religion of this culture would be the Southern Baptists and Presbyterians who knew how to interpret the Bible as the Word of God (and argue for the defense of slavery as intended by the scriptures). These Protestant churches were acknowledged and treated in ways similar to the "established" churches in the kingdoms (nation states) of Europe. This development in the deep South inadvertently changed the independent Protestant churches from Yankeedom into the semi-official state religion of the Southern block of states. They did not become "established" as the official religion of a Southern state on the model of the European nation states, but in the eyes of the people the village Baptist church served as the official religion of the state and represented the Protestant re-formation of the Catholic concept of Christendom. The anti-government Christian churches took their place as the foundation stones for the government of the Christian states in the South. It would not be long before they were asked to play that role for the United States as well. The radical transformation of Protestantism into a state religion had occurred.

From Reagan to the Bushes I and II the Republicans had been working on the plank of their platform in which Capitalism could be pursued as the reason for and the mythology of the government of the United States of America. This required the government to protect private enterprise and allow for the pursuit of private wealth without taxation. The Calvinist principle of salvation in which every individual was required to experience his/her own private conversion and make it certain by good works, and moral behavior, was based on a merger of capitalism with the Renaissance discovery of the individual person as the center of importance for the culture of a society. This merger had formed a new secular mythology of work ethic and reward that Max Weber studied to work out the relationship between Protestantism and Capitalism. He is the culture historian who had perceived the relation of Capitalism to the Protestant need to prove one's "salvation" by working hard and earning one's wages. Now the United States could be seen as the arena for private business and as a supervisor of the economy of private enterprise. It need not function any longer as the agency for overseeing the structural workings of the society as a whole or guaranteeing that the society worked well for all services and persons. The mythology of Protestant Capitalism was merging with the politics of the United States as the way to justify personal and private business and the acquisition of wealth. No wonder all of the Republican candidates for the presidency in 2016 went out of their way to assure their listeners that they were Christians. One wonders what Max Weber would say about this. What we now have is Protestantism turning into radical evangelical politics.

In the meantime, Obama was elected President and the term *Tea Party* was coined in Chicago as the way Republicans could keep Obama and the Democrats from "taxing" them in order to support the blacks, minorities, impoverished, and immigrant classes of society. The concept of welfare was no longer to be used. The concept of white male supremacy would now be the way in which the superiority of the United States would be authorized and guaranteed. Radical conservatives are now the leaders of what is called the Tea Party Republicans, and they are now in control of the political ideology that managed to elect Trump and lockdown both the Congress and the Supreme Court. As Chomsky describes Paul Ryan: "The few attempts to analyze his programs, after dispensing with the magic that is regularly introduced, conclude that his actual policies are to virtually destroy every part of the federal government that serves the interests of the general population, while expanding the military and ensuring that the rich and the corporate sector will be well attended to—the core Republican ideology when the rhetorical trappings are drawn aside (115)". Steve Bannon, another of Trump's advisors, has actually said much the same thing, namely, that he would like to see the entire Federal government and Democratic system torn down and replaced by what he calls "economic nationalism."

Critical Times for America

So now we have Trump planning to repeal the laws and tear down the agencies that have been set up to guarantee the welfare of planet earth and our society. The Democrats have been alert to the major threats of climate warming, corporate capitalism, nuclear war, and fascism. But given the metamorphoses of the traditional cultures toward *amnesia*, the transformation of Christianity into the me-ism of capitalism, and the shift from print media to social media and entertainment at the popular level of discourse, the Democrats have not been agile enough, or thoughtful enough, to propose an alternative program and agenda. And, there does not appear to be much chance for a culture historian to be heard amidst the noise. Chomsky says the Tea Party Republicans are rushing civilization to the cliff. As a lover of cabaret I immediately want to find the words for the final scene: "Where are the cameras?" But when "the cliff" is mentioned, it is fear, not humor, that pops up to sneer at thinking. Ending civilization in the violence of a self-imposed destruction does not seem to be an imaginable conclusion to our histories that makes sense. It immediately raises the question of the anthropology with which we have been working, the way in which we have thought about our *human nature*, why violence in the first place, and whether our inability to control violence will do us in. I therefore want to dedicate the next chapter to this issue. "The Causes of Human Aggression."

4

Social Anthropology
The Causes of Human Aggression

The United States is in the process of producing an ugly picture of its world. The ugliness is obvious in the media, the newspapers, videos, books, and magazines. The big picture at the local level includes drive-by shootings, black churches burning, police brutality, public demonstrations of white supremacists and Ku Klux Klan members, guns and gangs in the cities, and the sick, impoverished, and homeless peoples without help. At the level of the states there are high incarceration rates among blacks, deportations of other cultural peoples, industrial violations of ecosystems, native Americans pushed aside, and big oil allowed to drill for more even after we did not need any more. At the global level we have made unwelcomed intrusions into foreign countries, built military colonies around the world, arranged assassinations to topple "unfriendly" leaders, conducted wars against resistant tribes and sects abroad, and allowed massacres of peoples who get in the way of our pursuits of "national interests."

On the topic of guns and violence we have armed many parties in other lands to help them in their own pursuits of power for the control of their countries. The invariable result has been the formation of militias and police states to guarantee their control of the people and the "defense" of their land. We do not seem to notice that the armed conflicts throughout the so-called "third world" nations are a result of our own incursions and the selective distribution of arms to "leaders" thought to be friendly and cooperative in our global business enterprises. Our trade in arms is now big business, enough to keep our military and business relations with other nations strong in our favor. It has become a major factor in the "negotiations" of diplomatic relations. Given the role of European armaments in the wars and massacres in Europe in the last two centuries, we may not want to take all the credit for the global military chaos since the second world war. But the pattern we have created of military "missions" (intrusions) into other countries, the self-interested selection of "friendly" parties in other countries, and the distribution of American weapons to these friendly parties, is now the model used by other nations in their relations with neighboring countries. And especially since our incursions into the Middle East during the Bush II administration, the turmoil there shows no sign of "winning" any of the wars unleashed by any of the nations involved. The ugliness of this picture of nations at war, and societies in disorder and confusion as a result of these wars, is evident not only in the use of guns, gangs, armies, killings, and the violation of borders, cities, and monuments. The civil cultures among the peoples have become confused as well. In many countries the social atmosphere is no longer livable. Many of the societies we forced to become "democracies" are now societies that are fractured, tense, and frightening, with refugees fleeing and seeking places to live in other lands.

In America the daily patterns of intercourse are also in disarray, though without such obvious disruptions from foreign powers. We are fortunate that our dis-ease and disorder are not the direct result of foreign armies and drones attacking us as is the case in many other countries. But the tensions we have created with other nations under a self-righteous Bush and now an impulsive president have taken their toll on our sense of national security, and there is a mood of consternation that has begun to affect our thinking and discourse. There is consternation because (1) the president has threatened European agencies and foreign countries with his "America First" ideology and what he understands to be his "bigger button," because (2) the Republican Congress has shown itself to be obsequious to this president and is at work taking orders to dismantle the welfare state Democrats have built at least since FDR, and because (3) an offensive layer of odious personal talk and behavior has surfaced in the media and in politics now that Trump has unleashed a range of deeply seated undemocratic and uncivil prejudices to surface at the level of personal commands, behavior, and discourse that once were understood to be illicit and disgusting in the political arena. The layering of troubling behavior includes sexual obscenities, unjust economic predations, blindness to white male dominance, uncalled for anti-Jewish taunts, unlawful anti-black tirades, conceitful and deceitful political rhetoric, and the studied blindness of offensive anti-government groups like the Ku Klux Klan and White Supremacists, to say nothing of the president's own coterie who want to "crush" the Democrats and create an "economic nationalism" to "start over." Goodness. The yelling at one another and the obscenities targeting groups of protesters are now a feature of the daily news, including persons in Washington, the film industry, and of course the social media. As a matter of fact, persons in all departments of the government have also been charged with unacceptable attitudes and behavior, many choosing to retire in order to avoid trial or retribution. The surge of charges about sexual harrassment in a working area, for instance, to take only one of the features of our distasteful picture, while astounding as the revelation of a wide-spread index of social violence and dis-ease, is far from the only revelation about the social mentality that is upsetting. The daily news about the #MeToo phenomenon is upsetting because it somehow fits with other features of our social miasma, including the emergence of white males who openly acknowledge and parade their "supremacy," a focus on inordinate wealth as the mark of greatness, and the Tea Party lockdown in Washington that has no real concern to care for the social agencies and structures required for the well-being of the people. As the party whose only platform is to guarantee wealth for the rich, and whose strategies turn into public displays of conceit and deceit, the Tea Party Republicans must remain silent in the face of this social chaos, for they actually have nothing constructive to say. Their silence, however, is not innocent. That is because, as the party whose objective has been to dismantle the social welfare of the advancements of the Democrats and the Obama administration, they do not have an alternative constructive platform to tell the public what they are for. What they want, they have said, is to repeal Obamacare and "crush" (Bannon's word) the social Democrats and their Federal government in the interest of "Greatness Again," meaning more wealth for the rich. The Republicans have revealed a mentality that is self-righteous, single-minded, racist, and anti-feminist in a world that is multicultural and weary of male superiority and the use of force to govern and control a people.

The problem perceived by the people is that the government has failed to care for the under and middle classes on the one hand, and the use of politics and police force to guarantee law and order on the other. The events of killings and human aggression fall somewhere in the middle without being addressed as a social illness. The question raised on all fronts by protest demonstrations, progressive movements, and political party reorganizations, is how to address social distress when the current government fails to listen. There is also a sense in which the people in general, as well as the officials in government, have learned to take the incidence of discord, anger, and violence for granted. That is because the patterns of conflict and defence now in place all assume that, if a conflict is not resolved by other means, the conflict can easily eventuate *naturally* in violence. And the short list of examples given above can all be reduced to the question of why such is occurring in our modern society at the end of Western civilization.

Taking the problem of "shootings" as an obvious example of our distress, there is currently a marked increase in shootings in schools that kill numbers of students. We usually know who the shooter was, and the media starts with an investigation of the perpetrator, thinking that the individual must have had reasons for the behavior. Then the person's relationship to the victims and their recent histories requires attention. And finally, the circumstances need to be investigated, including the source of any weapons used, the occasion and its potential for turning the violence into some kind of statement, and any notes or clues sent to family and friends. Several suspicions usually surround these matters such as racial tensions, religious prejudice, occupational history, and whether the person had earlier run-ins with the law. When all of that is cleared up, judgments are possible about the individual's motivation, guilt or innocence, and whether the action was planned, accidental, or impulsive. And that seems to be enough for the family, police, and the courts.

But after reading the news on such scenes day after day, the thought occurs that all the questions have not been asked, much less answered. What about the fact that this type of unacceptable behavior has become a common event in the society? Is it not possible to ask other kinds of why questions about that common occurrence? If so, our response to such an occurrence has to shift from considerations of particular personal motivations to pensive reflection on the state of the society as a whole and its possible involvement in the circumstances surrounding the event. What is it about our society that allows such events of violence to occur? The customary answer to this question has been first to look for features of the particular circumstance that may have triggered the violence, but then to say something to the effect that, since such features are common occurrences, they cannot have been the cause of this particular incident. This round of argumentation can take place at a fairly high level of reflection, commentary, and debate about the social occurrences common to a society, but it seldom engages the question of why a *society* "thinks" and works that way. These are questions we have not adequately conceptualized as a people, or even framed. Given the seriousness of the issues involved, however, these questions will not go away without some consideration of our culture's mentalities and values. This chapter will attempt to address the issue of our social values and mentality that play a role in support of the events of violence that have become standard features of our histories.

But first, there is a common answer to these questions about violence that calls upon theories of evolution and ethology, one of the few attempts to discover the logic of a social phenomenon, this one in respect to the incidence of violence. It needs to be mentioned and set aside. The theories in question are intended to explain the common events of killings and violence, and to suggest ways to respond, but they actually make the picture of violence in our society even more ugly and much more difficult to understand. They lodge in a stream of discourse among ethologists and evolutionists to the effect that humans have been *naturally* aggressive since the beginning of the species, and that aggression and killing are human instincts that have become "hard wired" in our brains and embedded in our genes. This theory had its origin in the study by Konrad Lorenz, *Das sogenannte Boese* (Methuen, 1963), translated as *On Aggression* (1966). Lorenz was an ethologist known for his study of the behavior of birds, focusing on Greylag Geese. It was a thorough investigation of what at that time was understood as ritual behavior. Lorenz's thesis was that the ritual behavior of Greylag Geese was a form of communication, and that it was a complex set of signals used to attract a mate and strike a bond necessary for raising a family. A few ritual theorists in sociology and cultural anthropology found Lorenz's work intriguing because it seemed to answer questions about the function of early human (tribal) rituals that were still unclear. This was considered a great advance in ethnological studies interested in the question of what ritual ("religion") contributed to early human social formations. Lorenz himself contributed to this discussion by taking a leap from the geese to the human to explain that ritual communication among humans was the way in which the consequences of threat, offense, hostility and violence were acknowledged and addressed. He must have had the Christian ritual of Christ's "sacrifice" in mind, the basic symbol of "communication" for

Catholic Christianity, and the means by which offenses and their rectifications could take place, though he does not say so.

For the historian of religion, this overlay of disciplines from ethology, ethnography, theology, and cultural anthropology was startling. Biblical scholars were well aware that the story of Jesus's crucifixion was indebted to the concept of martyrdom which the Greeks had applied to various political killings in the Greco-Roman world, a concept that was not at first understood as a "sacrifice" either by Hebrews or Greeks, but more as a hero tale with connotations about the importance of the martyr's ideology and stance within the political situation and the social circumstances that pertained. When the early Christians such as Paul used the term *sacrifice* to interpret the earlier story of Jesus's martyrdom, they did so in order to establish a link between Jesus and God, and thus between the new grouping of Jesus people and the Hebrews, drawing upon the Hebrew Scriptures and the temple system of sacrifices for the rectification of wrong doings. The reader might well consult Rom 3:25 ("whom God put forth as a sacrifice of atonement"); Rom 8:3 ("by sending his own son in the likeness of sinful flesh as a sin offering"); 1 Cor 5:7 ("for our paschal lamb, Christ, has been sacrificed"); and 1John 4:10 ("sent his son to be the atoning sacrifice for our sins"). It was this use of the term *sacrifice* that became the primary descriptor for the meaning of the Christ myth and its ritual in Catholic Christianity. It is this ritual and its importance for Christian theology that became the source of the concept and widespread use of the term in the Western traditions of literature, philosophy, and, since Lorenz, comparative ethnography. This concept of "sacrifice" in Christian mythology was not acknowledged or picked up in the subsequent discourse of the Lorenz debates. It was, however, not long before the many rituals in which an "offering" was made or a killing of some kind took place, that ethnographers and cultural anthropologists began using the term sacrifice. Such rituals in both tribal and other non-Christian religions and societies could then be explained as the way in which they sublimated aggressive instincts in the interest of more humanizing motivations. A flurry of treatises and essays on the part of culture analysts found this theory to be not only "true", because it bridged between science and religion, but also because it provided an answer to a range of questions about humans and their societies that still needed to be asked. The list of scholars writing about ritual in this vein is long, but the primary authors and titles include Robert Ardrey, *African Genesis* (1961); Desmond Morris, *The Naked Ape* (1967); and Anthony

Social Anthropology

Storr, *Human Aggression* (1968). These writings were quickly taken up by many others as if an important consensus had been reached in social anthropology that could explain the reasons for the violence that was beginning to be noticed as a feature of Western societies.

Ashley Montagu, English-American anthropologist, found this discourse troubling and made a thorough study of the claims that were being made by these scientists and social historians. In 1976 he published *The Nature of Human Aggression* (Oxford) in which he took this collection of scholars to task. It is a lengthy essay (381 pages) taking up all of the theoretical terms that cropped up in this discourse, such as "instinct," embedded in our "genes," therefore "ineradicable," as well as those that traced the history and origins of aggression to the "original moments" when humans created weapons for hunting, defense, and killing one another. Montagu summed up the views of this consensus held by his opponents:

> Humans are violent creatures in their most fundamental nature. They are naturally killers . . . it was through the invention of weapons—tools for killing—that pre-human creatures became human . . . that humankind's aggressiveness is powered by a spontaneous force, a kind of energy that builds inexorably within each of us and that must be periodically discharged . . . that being aggressive we are also territorial, characterized by an instinct of territorial defense inherited from our animal ancestors, and stronger and more compelling than sex as a motivating force. Hence: war between nations.[1]

I was in Germany during this debate, studying with Hans Conzelmann at the University of Göttingen. I had become interested in the origins of the Christian Myth, and mentors at the San Francisco Theological Seminary said that Conzelmann was at work on the history of Christian Origins, and that I should study with him. I had no idea about what I might find there. In keeping with the German university's practice of openness to the sciences and humanities, as well as its rigor in the pursuit of specialized studies (disciplines), on the one hand, and in the context of the post-Hitler confusion and pensiveness of the German people, on the other, the reader may imagine that the departments of Bible and theology were well aware of the Konrad Lorenz debates at the time. Without direct reference to this debate there were a number of major shifts in what they called New Testament Theology. It was the time for Rudolf Bultmann's program for

---

1. Montagu, *Nature of Human Aggression*, 7–8.

"demythologization," the attempt to translate Paul's "Christ Myth" (1 Cor 15:3–6) into existentialist, human, secular concepts, and thus cancel out thinking about the myth as the mythologization of an historical event, or a theological statement about "Christ's sacrifice." It was also the time for many attempts to understand other texts of New Testament times as documents of the "history of religions" rather than theological systems. This was understood as a study of the "background" or cultural context of Christian origins, thus an attempt to counter the "theological interpretation" of the New Testament and its mythic claim upon Christian mentality. These included the texts from Egypt, the ancient Near East, Greece, Rome, and many from the Greco-Roman cultures that had broken away from older patriarchal, monarchical understandings of peoples and their religions. And the new understandings began to treat the stories of the gods much like fictions, despite the fact that many had become central symbols for a particular configuration of people (such as the "mystery religions") or a special occasion for a traditional people (such as the celebration of the Eleusinian Mysteries or the *Athenaia*). All of these expansions of the horizon for Biblical and theological studies were driven by the new interests in the social histories of human existence. These newer social interests had not yet settled upon a social definition or theory of the human, staying at the level of descriptive social behavior and practice, but it was a sharp and enlightening switch from a theology accustomed to working with categories taken from within the mythic world of the Bible and treated as "historical". And now there was a set of hypotheses that addressed the *nature* of the human by means of analogies from ethology, thus bridging from the human to the animal, and the present to the "origins" of a particularly evident and troubling characteristic: violence. The Göttingen theologians were taking the primary categories of Western Philosophy such as time/space, human/animal, society/war, violence/redemption, in a radically new set of combinations in order to propose a new anthropology (view of the human at the level of social and primary character traits).

Conzelmann wanted to stay at the level of social description until we could be sure that all features of the Christ-myth texts were accounted for, including Jesus as the son of God, the last supper, the crucifixion, his resurrection, and ascension. They were to be accounted for in terms of the Greco Roman resources available, using what we now call "analogies" to find other times and places where various images, themes, and textual traditions could be seen to have crossed. He was also a multiculturalist in thinking that every one of the "resources," from all of the cultures impinging upon Christian origins, had to be researched in order to be sure. He sent me to study the ancient Near Eastern literature looking for analogies to what was then thought to be the "wisdom myth" of the ancient Near East as the "background" to both the Christ Myth and the Prologue to John's Gospel. It took me two and a half years, and I did not find any "wisdom myth" until I got to the Wisdom of Solomon (a first-century BCE Hellenistic Jewish text) and Philo of Alexandria (first-century CE Hellenistic Jewish biblical commentator or essayist). I cheated with these two, taking more time with them because of the obvious presence of a wisdom myth in both, and its further translation into a mythology of the *logos* ("word," "reason") in Philo. Conzelmann found it interesting that I had not found any precursors to the wisdom myth or the Christ myth in the texts of the ancient Near East and said that I should write it up. I knew that my study had helped to confirm his thesis about the Egyptian analogies for the wisdom myth and the primary features of the early Christian mythologies, but that I would have to wait for his own considered reflections on the big question still outstanding, namely the basic anthropology at work in such a cultural mixture and translation. I am afraid he died before getting *that* "written up." So I had to take Lorenz along on the next step of my own quest, now to the study of myth in ethnology.

But first, back to Montagu. He was an eminent anthropologist who had to take on the huge data base from ethnography that was building up. He did not like the way in which the many scientists and social historians so quickly took advantage of Lorenz's theory to support the standard notions of human aggression and violence, namely that they were "natural," i.e. in the "genes" or "brain wiring," and thus could not be remedied. The only thing to be done, in their view, was to make laws against violent behavior and provide police and military units to force compliance. This attitude was widespread and implicitly provided "reasons" for war and violence, and for rejecting the criticisms of war by what conservatives called "softies" and "socialists." Montagu's survey of the ethnological data base (tribal societies) found many tribes that eschewed violence and killing, and that had found ways to reprimand individuals who occasionally may have acted that way. In some cases in my own reading of ethnography, a "reprimand" would take the form of a parody performed by others to make fun of a person or couple publically. And in general, there were many human societies that had values we now call "empathy," "loyalty," "cooperation," and "honors," with no thought of these as necessary in order to ward off violence. In fact, the notion of belonging to a tribe as a "community" was not special at all, much less entertained as a counter argument against violence. The values of belonging to a community were *learned* (Montagu's emphasis) in the process of caring for children and being cared for as children, and in the many events of living together as families and tribes ("Watch. This is how you do it."). These relational experiences and values were all assumed without having to be turned into conscious rules of behavior. What a thought! There was no need for Montagu to offer an argument against the findings of ethology per se, or against the functions of the human anatomy called upon by others to ground Lorenz's theory. It was the ease with which two scientific disciplines (ethology and biology) had been used to support a modern *cultural* understanding of violence that Montagu found wanting. And so, toying with the title of his book, his thesis is that *The Nature of Human Aggression* is not *natural*. One might worry a bit about a sociologist having to get so involved to argue against a common consensus among social scientists, a consensus focused upon the *individual* instead of on the social in order to investigate the society's practices. But the arguments in favor of Lorenz and his theory of violence were all set forth by scholars and thinkers who were innocently working with modern cultural notions about the violence of individuals and so had to be addressed at that level. Montagu would not be moved. It was precisely the use of misguided ethology and unproven biology as arguments *for* the violence in our society that needed to be addressed and countered.

So, if violence is not "natural," why does it happen? This is the why question that needs to be answered. Earlier in this essay the why question was being asked by the media about individuals and particular events. All of their answers assumed that the objective was to determine the guilt or the innocence of the perpetrator. Once that was determined the case could be closed. There was nothing about the social circumstances surrounding the event or the underlying logic of the culture that may have assumed violence was natural, leaving unaddressed the question about why, then, there is so much anger, rage, and violence outbreaking at this particular time in our society. This question needs a frame of reference larger than an evolutionary theory brought to focus on individual actors. It requires the acknowledgment and assessment of the history of American society to unravel a number of ideologies, social interests and practices that have become features of the culture. It is not just the "shooters" that are acting out of mental distress. It is our society that is sliding into a mental derangement of social behavior and discourse. It is the mood and ambience of the social order that is creating dis-ease and frustration for all of us as individuals, but especially for our youth and those who have no intellectual recourse to situations of stress, discipline, unemployment, and confused cultural identity that the society has caused. How can that be?

Woodard's dialectic of Individualism and Communitarianism as the two streams of social values that have characterized the history of our eleven nations, values that he was able to trace throughout in terms of political and economic conflicts, can be used to clarify the fundamental issue. It is that the Communitarian vision of the New England nations has been overwhelmed by the cultivation of the freedom of the individual. The French and American revolutionary notions of freedom included that of both individuals and governments; individuals from oppressive rulers and governments, and governments from oppressive hierarchies and traditions. In America the freedom of the individual was able to develop as the major pole of the dialectic, and become the definition of America as the "Land of the Free." In course, the notion of freedom was merged with the logics of capitalism and trading to define the freedom of our financial institutions from government, and to define our Democracy as the way in which "free trade" was protected. And both capitalism and democracy are preoccupied with individualism, thus accounting for the demise of the communitarian vision of society. Woodard's judgment is that the United States is the "most individualistic" nation ever. He accounts for it by tracing the history of the nations in his second book on the subject, *The American Character*, and noting the roles played by the politicians and policies of every nation in their quest of independence from taxation, government control, and the interests of the other nations.

Picking up on Montagu's image of "the family" as the fundamental formation of human tribal society, the complex set of relationships and values that an individual "learns" by belonging to that social unit such as interest in the tribe as a family, knowing one's place and role in the family and tribe, and caring about what others think and do (including what we now call empathy), the short answer to our question about why then there is so much aggression in our society is that our nation has not evolved as a family that thinks and behaves in terms of a shared social interest, identity, and mythology. It is not even a single nation on the model of the European nations from which our eleven separate "nations" (Woodard's term) evolved as "colonies."

Critical Times for America

America is a set of "states" derived from different colonies that were forced to "unite" (against British forces) in the course of a rather long period of frustration with the desire of the British for dominance over their colonies abroad. The colonies became a federation by means of reaching compromises among themselves, calling a series of congresses, then a constitution, and agreeing upon the "need" to take up arms against the British when the king did not come to terms with them. Each colony brought along the social configurations and nuances of the country it left behind, together with its religious, political, and ethnographic cultures. The history of America that Woodard reviews, reveals multiple incidents of fierce disagreements among the colonies and eventual states, threats to each other as colonies, and appeals to the federal government as if it were responsible to solve perceived violations of a given colony's pattern of practices and basic identity issues. Some formed militias during the French and Revolutionary wars, and there were several skirmishes and wars with other colonies in the attempt to solve disagreements. We also have a history of attempts at secession until forced to comply with the federal coalition. On the expansions to the West each colony-nation moved more or less as a single people to populate large swaths of territory without much mixing with those of the other nations. What eventually developed as a more or less common concept of the "United States" was indeed a culture, but one that had only two basic values, one of "freedom" and the other of "individualism." America became the land of the free individuals. Woodard says that there is no other nation in the world that is so individualistic in its self-understanding as America.

In earlier studies of mythic mentality and the social orders of collective interests I became impressed with what I understood as the fading of the Christian myth from its erstwhile control of religious institutions, and from its influence on the secular worlds of cultural arts and productions. Tracking the changes that had been made in the thinking of the people by the rise of the Renaissance in the fourteenth to sixteenth centuries, the Reformation in the sixteenth century, the Enlightenment in the seventeenth to eighteenth centuries, and Capitalism since the eighteenth and nineteenth centuries, I finally found myself engaged by what social and cultural historians were calling the *postmodernism* of the twentieth century. This was a term used to suggest that the grand tradition of Western thinking had come to its end, and that the era of late capitalism, multiculturalism, electronic media, and virtual reality no longer had interest in the academic traditions of philosophy, history, and the arts. I discussed this in *The Rise and Fall of the Christian Myth* in a section called "Cultural Analytics" where the studies by David Harvey (*The Condition of Postmodernism*) and Frederic Jameson (*The Political Unconscious: Narrative as a Socially Symbolic Act*) described the thoroughly individualistic and subjective ambiance of the "new age", leaving no room for the history or religions (201–24). This helped to understand the fading of what I had called the "big picture" of a people's world, religion, and its myth, especially in the case of Catholic Christendom that had projected a universalistic and cosmic worldview. And since my big picture theory of the Christian myth started with the cosmic worldview of Christendom, but then had been brought down to the level of human history in the Reformation, it allowed a Protestant reading of the Bible as an epic history from creation to the apocalypse that gave the Christ event in the middle its significance as the pivot of a universal (anthropological) history and the sign of Christianity as the "chosen people" with a mission to convert the other nations of the world. Thus the dialectic of the two orders of the human race, the righteous (Christian) nation, and the "unwashed" pagan peoples, that seemed to be the major factor in self-understanding of the American people as special and superior.

But that vision of the Christian myth did not fully fade, even though the "mission" to the world was now a matter of cultural invasion and military power. This means that the Bible as epic history seemed to be fading from the consciousness of the American people, even as the concept of the Christian "mission" was being translated in terms of the "leadership" of the "Christian Nation" in the global world. Since Trump, I needed to ask whether there was anything else being "translated" instead of erased that might help account for the failure of our missions and the anger underlying modern mentality? Enter the study by Susan Mizruchi, Professor of English and American Studies at Boston University, with the title: *The Science of Sacrifice* (1998). Mizruchi's project was to determine the relationship between literature and society, similar in some ways to my own attempts to find the links between Christian myth and social formations. As a professor of English literature, she was thoroughly engaged with the reading of the many nineteenth- and twentieth-century authors in this field and discipline, pondering how authors looked at their societies, and how their writings described it in the genre of novels, poems, mini essays, fictions, and so forth. Literature became a layer of social thought marked by a loosely knit class of very intelligent and skilled intellectuals who found themselves curious about some feature of their society that was troubling and used an art-form to describe it and write about it as an analysis that could be read and studied by other readers and authors. Mizruchi's quest was to understand the thinking that linked American literature and social science. But, as she puts it in her "Introduction", she stumbled upon "religion" as a "third element" that linked social science and literature in the "deep structure of sacrificial rites" and so formed "border texts" in the interstices between the sciences and the arts. She used this insight to organize her book on "Sacrificial Arts and Sacrifices" (Chapter One), "The Return to Sacrifice in Melville and Others" (Chapter Two), "Rites of Passage in an Awkward Age" (Chapter Three), and "Du Bois's Gospel of Sacrifice" (Chapter Four). Emile Durkheim and "the British Bible Specialists" are mentioned repeatedly throughout the 436 pages. And at this level of cultural sense and sensibility the biblical images of sacrifices, including the scapegoat, the anti-killing "sacrifice" of Isaac, and the redemptive crucifixion of the Christ, are found to be enmeshed at the "deep level" of linkage between society and culture. Mizruchi unrolls this deep structure of thought through 436 pages of very profound readings of the writings and social contexts of the entire history of English literature. Wonderful analyses are given for the plots in Melville's *Moby Dick* and *Billy Budd, Sailor;* also for Du Bois's studies of lynching and *The Souls of Black Folk*; as well as of the works of Weber, Durkheim and many other culture analysts and biblical scholars. In every case it is the concept and image of sacrifice that draws their narratives of a social issue to its "fitting" conclusion providing "an accurate summary of sacrificial transactions". "The social is defined by what is *given up* in order to reproduce it" (Introduction, 23. Italics in the original). The result of Mizruchi's demonstration of "the dominance of sacrifice as a social practice ... (and) the relevance of sacrifice as social thought and social action" (Introduction, 23) is that my "fading" of the Christian myth now needs to be seen mainly in the loss of the cosmic worldview and the conscious articulation of the symbols of Christendom in the practices and institutions of the modern postmodern society. But at the deep levels of sensibility and understanding, where the social psychology of mythic images continues to inform the way we think about social issues and decisions, the concept of sacrifice is the major image and rationale for stories that engage social issues.

Before proceeding to a consideration of the way in which the current situation of social issues is being handled in this vein, we might want to notice that, in the case of the Christian myth with its sacrifice of the Christ, the marks a violent death count as "good" for god and his believers. For

Social Anthropology

those who do not accept or believe the Christ myth, there is the threat of violence in the apocalyptic ending of history and the judgment to take place at the end of their own lives. And as the cosmic worldview has receded, the social arena has inadvertently become the canvas where the working out of the social narrative takes place in terms of the myth. This has been exacerbated in America by the rising of Individualism to the positions of the power and authority of the strong man who now takes it upon himself to act in the roles of king, priest, and savior. The gospel now provides the rationale for social transactions and purposes. The Christ myth is still the basic narrative informing social transactions, but it is capitalism that wins in the social arena where the strong man can sacrifice others in the execution of corporate interests.

This is not a happy thought for humanists, liberals, Christian communitarians, or socialists. It has therefore been possible for biblical scholars to start with the widespread analogy of "sacrifice" as a religious ritual among human communities and then argue for the "truly exceptional" Christian myth in which it was god, himself who "sent his Son as a sacrifice" for humans and offered redemption. This ups the ante on the mythic basis for "sacrifice," but without explanation, and it does not acknowledge that it is the Christian term *sacrifice* that has become a common definition of many non-Christian rituals in which an "offering" or a "killing" takes place. It is the importance of the term "sacrifice" to Christianity (as the definition of the crucifixion of the "Christ Event") that has turned the actions and significance of many rituals, both Christian and non-Christian into a "sacrifice." Thus the underlying logic for both the Christ myth and the use of the term *sacrifice* in social anthropology has no other concept or definition in Western philosophy and discourse. The term is actually used as a matter of familiarity with the Christian theological system, even though not acknowledged. It is as if the term suggests that there must be some logic to it based in the spiritual, cosmic, divine realm which is, of course, unavailable for scientific investigation. For the church and its theologians that has seemed to confirm the truth of its transcendent source and logic by means of strange mental gymnastics that wants to use metaphor and virtual reality as arguments for the truth of mythic applications to historical reality. For the academic, however, it is that feature of a mythic symbol which calls for social analysis. People who resist the cultural critique of the American (Western) mythic mentality cannot be charged with a stubborn resistance to the truth, as if, seeing the issue clearly, they have decided to remain ignorant. The myth of a people and its communitarian significance is a matter of identity and belonging, very basic and deep sensibilities without which a person cannot function. The rejection of a cultural critique is not a matter of intelligence failure and faulty decision. It is a matter of not having any other place to be and see that another frame of reference is possible. Thus the question invariably turns the focus back around to ask about the social mentality that resides in the myth at the basis of the society. Social mentality is also difficult to posit for analysis, but it is available for investigation at the level of the habitual behavior practices of a people. The people are always aware of these practices, whether as perfectly in keeping with the mythic norms, or as personal affronts and aggressions that usually call for some response. It is in the give and take of the living together and its common discourse, that insights are achieved in the social logic of the shared mentality. Such situations and insights are the places where shifts can be detected, if not encouraged, that indicate awareness of the social logics involved. We will have to take this insight up again in chapter five, where the American distrust of the concept of a multicultural social democracy has to be addressed.

The failures of our society and its leaders to recognize such issues and respond to them creatively still rankle our educated youth, especially since the Viet Nam War (1960s and 70s). Our youth do not escape the general sense of America's inability to address political issues and to consider the consequences of weak political parties that have no answer to the stagnation of the economy, the gap between the rich and the poor, the erosion of the American Dream, the high cost of education, the rise of homelessness, climate warming, the lack of medical insurance and health care for all, to say nothing about the resurrection of nuclear war as a threat. And currently there is a single issue political party in Washington that has created an aggravating lock down in all departments of the government. This is the Republican party which has been working against the modest attempts of the Democrats to create a common-good welfare society. Reagan shut down the funding for mental care because the mentally ill were not the responsibility of the state. Under Bill Clinton the Democrats became Neoliberals, cooperating with Wall Street and overlooking the problems they were creating for middle class wage earners. The inauguration of Obama was an exhilarating change in the political climate, and many of us thought that he might be able to rectify the picture of foreign wars and state-capitalism that the Republicans had painted. But No. Obama was not only a Democrat; he was a black man. The Republican Congress dug in its heels and, on the trading floor of the Chicago Mercantile Exchange, the CNBC personality Rick Santelli made a speech denouncing Obama's "welfare" attempts to help homeowners endangered by the housing crisis (mostly black), denouncing those in danger of foreclosure as "losers," and calling for "The Tea Party" to resist the Obama presidency. Republicans did indeed resist and form The Tea Party, some yelling at the president from the floor of Congress, calling him a liar, others simply turning their backs and walking out when he was presiding. And among the electorate there were activists galore brandishing racist signs and slogans smearing Obama and black people, and telling Obama to go back to Kenya, etc. On the way to the end of his terms, the Tea Party organized the most single issue political party imaginable. In their minds the standard Republican fixation on "No new taxes" devolved into a single platform that said "No" to everything Obama and the Democrats wanted to do, and called for a government shut down if their own position on repealing Obamacare and dismantling Democratic welfare agencies was violated.

It should not be surprising, then, that the Republican candidates for the presidency were all Christians and fell into line behind Trump's showmanship of making America Great Again on the basis of hostility attacks on Democrats, opponents, and foreign nations. Nor should it be surprising that his ugly campaign against Hillary did not keep him from "winning" the election. The campaign against both opponents, Obama as predecessor and Hillary as a woman, was egregiously racist and white male supremacist, even if both prejudices did not actually become obvious to the public until after the Women's March at the Inauguration and Trump's contemptuous refusal to answer criticisms of the Charlottesville white supremacists' rally. The media have added many more items to the list of Trump's contemptuous twitters in the course of his first year as president. We need not review them. The American people are finally waking up to the fact that Trump's behavior has alienated the international community of nations, and that his Tea Party Congress and administration has already done deep damage to our nation and its future. His cohorts, given assignments in charge of the government's agencies, have already begun to threaten America's commitments to nuclear disarmament, international climate control, NATO, The United Nations, UNESCO, and other treaties with the European nations. The youth of America are not dumb. They may have been deprived of an honest history of America that was needed to understand the social logics involved in the devolution of our political visions, but they are well aware of the government's lack of interest in the health and well-being of the society and its inability to understand the issues of injustice, inequity, and insecurity for all people.

The shooting in Parkland, Florida, on February 14, 2018, can be used as an example of the reasons our society has for its anxiety and anger. The Parkland school shooting killed seventeen people. Students and others were frightened, then enraged. The social media was flooded with anger at yet another school shooting and the failure of the government to do anything about our lack of gun control. Students started marching toward government offices. They wrote speeches and requested conferences with school officials, the police, and the NRA. They wanted to know why we still had no gun control. The media found that their protest was so obviously right and reasonable, that they had actually reintroduced the topic of gun control which had languished, and the tenor of the national and international news joined the students in demanding that all concerned respond. The President's response was in character, the offer of money to train and equip a million teachers to have guns. He was not going to stand by and leave "his schools" undefended. The social media went wild, not able to find anything in the president's attitude, character, or thinking that made any sense at all. It treated the students and schools as "his" property, juveniles to be defended and cared for, as if they needed to be defended from gunmen all around who could be expected to act like gunmen at any time. It merely echoed the statement of Wayne LaPierre, CEO of the NRA, after the shooting in Newtown, Connecticut in 2012: "The only way to stop a bad guy with a gun is with a good guy with a gun." So what we need is more guns. Now, days after the Parkland shooting, the CEO was upset with the protesters who wanted gun control and the media who were criticizing the National Rifle Association for its pro-gun political policies. They are "socialists," he said, "What they want are more restrictions on the law-abiding . . . Think about that," he told the Conservative Political Action Conference. "Their solution is to make you, all of you, less free . . . If they seize power . . . our American freedoms could be lost and our country will be changed forever . . . Socialism is a movement that loves a smear . . . The Second Amendment staunchly defends every American's right to bear arms."

So there we have the responses of the President of the United States and a leading business man and CEO, spouting out their prejudices in anger as gospel truth. We should stop long enough to notice (1) that a military mentality is involved in the attack and defends arguments about having guns, (2) that the conservatives' misreading of the Second Amendment is about an *individual's* "right to bear arms," not the historical reasons for a *state* to have a "militia" during the Revolutionary War, (3) that "socialism" is now considered an enemy of the conservatives' political agenda, as well as a threat to the American nation, and (4) that if the protestors and their socialist supporters were to "seize power," using the terms of revolutionary warfare, it would be the end of our "American freedoms." This atrocious response of our "leaders" to the questions they were asked by the student protesters reveals the mentality of those in charge of our country in general. Notice that several items of our "character" as underscored by Woodard are put forth simply as self-evident. America is for *individuals*. Individuals should be *free*. The *right* to be free and have a gun is granted in the Constitution. The *welfare* and *protection* of the people are nowhere in sight. Those who *protest* are enemies of America. And *socialism* is a movement that wants to restrict our freedoms. Should the *socialists seize power* our freedoms will be lost and our country changed forever.

It does not take an inordinate reading of history to recognize that statements such as these describe a fascist mentality of the need to curb or destroy the proletariat in the interest of a dictator's power, law, and order. It tells us that the Republicans have lost their vision of America as a social democracy, and that that may be the reason for their anti-democratic postures in Washington and throughout their worlds of wealth, Wall Streets, international corporations, anti-immigration policies, anti-communitarian attitudes, and refusals to join with other nations such as NATO, the UN, and the European Union in their concerns for planet earth and nuclear disarmament. Trump's "Great" and "First" is all about Military Power and Money. And we wonder why there is so much anger, aggression, and killing?

In one of the last chapters of the Noam Chomsky book on *Optimism over Despair: On Capitalism, Empire, and Social Change*, his interviewer C. J. Polychroniou, asks him "Is the United States Ready for Socialism?" The answer basically is that, if we are not, the Republicans win and the ugliness gets worse until we go over the cliff. To use this metaphor is frightening, of course. But it is also called for by the state of the world America has created. The list of social issues I have enumerated on several occasions in other books has not yet included the problem of population growth that Paul and Anne Ehrlich, Stanford University scientists, have been working on for fifty years. A recent review of this work by Damian Carrington bears the title: "Collapse of Civilization is a Near Certainty within Decades" (*Guardian*,

March 22, 2018). Quoting Ehrlich, "It is a near certainty in the next few decades, and the risk is increasing continually as long as perpetual growth of the human enterprise remains the goal of economic and political systems ... As I've said many times, 'perpetual growth is the creed of the cancer cell.'" Damian Carrington continues: "It is the combination of high population and high consumption by the rich that is destroying the natural world ... this is driving a sixth mass extinction of biodiversity upon which civilization depends for clean air, water and food."

This is yet another example of the possibility that our cleverness and corporate pursuits, products of Western civilization, have yet to recognize the physical and social limits of our capitalistic drives. The last five hundred years have seen the most glorious evolution of the human mind, intelligence, and creativity. But the Western mind has not discovered the *values* of social existence and the cultural creativities that could enhance it in ways that would make it rewarding to live together without needing wealth, power, or violence. Using the customary Republican response to such an idea, "it would cost too much." So the cliff metaphor needs to be expanded to include nuclear war, climate disaster, planet earth atrophy, stock market crash, mass food poisoning, and other similar threatening scenarios. All of these are examples of Mizruchi's discovery of sacrifice as a social thought and action.

In the next chapter I want to argue for a social democracy as our best bet at the end of the Western tradition of civilization and culture, "best bet" meaning learning to live together on planet earth without killing one another, i.e. without aggression.

5

Social Democracy
Intelligence or Power

Our ugly picture needs repainting. It will not be easy, but it must be done. That is because the picture we now have before us is not only ugly, it reveals a people in anger and a future that is frightening. The anger and fear do not commend themselves as an atmosphere conducive for constructive activity and a sense of well-being. The use of the term *picture* is a metaphor, of course, and the idea of *repainting* it can easily lead to misunderstandings if the metaphor itself is misunderstood. I coined the term *big picture* while working with ethnographers in a quest for the social function of myth and ritual in tribal societies. It seemed clear that the public performances of myths and rituals were social occasions as well as ways of remembering the people's place in their imagined world. They were social occasions in the sense that the rehearsal of a myth was a formal remembrance of a precedent event, and that a ritual was related to the performance of a regular practice of some significance to the way the tribe was organized and worked together (such as hunting, herding, or harvesting). The term *worldview* was one of the ways ethnographers talked about the fact that all people took the *world* in which they lived for granted.

This worldview could be imagined as a picture painted on a big canvas in which two environments were combined, the terrain or natural order, and the social history of the tribe. I used the term *big picture*, rather than *worldview*, as a way to incorporate both the worldscape and the tribal history on a single screen. This metaphor worked fairly well for tribal people, the ancient Near Eastern kingdoms, the Greeks, and even the history of Western Civilization (Christendom) with its cosmic mythology and epic history that centered the society in the Church, and the Church at the center of the biblical history derived from the Bible. Then, however, the Renaissance challenge to its mythology and the Reformation challenge to its social history resulted in the break up of its comprehensiveness, sufficiency, and cohesion as the big picture had to make room for the cluster of human projects and European kingdoms that emerged. For the last three hundred years we have not had a coherent worldview of the big picture kind. Chapter 1 has surveyed the social and intellectual distress of the European zone in the aftermath of the ending of Christendom. In Chapter 2 Woodard has retold the story of the social conflicts and confusing categories in the histories of the eleven American nations, and explained why America has not been able to form a *United* States, much less a picture of the Union that Woodard calls "Communitarian." In both arenas, European and American, it is the fragmentation of the big picture of Christendom that makes the quest for a principle of authority (Chapter 1) and the search for a compromise between individualism and communitarianism (Chapter 2) necessary themes.

The medieval picture was cosmic in scope and shape, packed full with the Christian imagery of the Christ event and Biblical history. It did not have space or place for the many figures and events of human discoveries and inventions that began to encroach upon the screen with other figures and memories. We need not go into detail about all the discoveries and inventions that occurred in the history of the Western Tradition, or about all the projects that were produced under the topics of the arts, literature, science, industry, education, business, empire, and the abolutely astounding globalization of finance, media, and the electronic world that is today the major supplier of what used to be the news. I have traced some of that history in recent publications, and write now to acknowledge the significance of the American chapter of the Western story since the Second World War, and to confess the intellectual confusion it has wrought, especially since the Trump campaign and presidency. The point must be made that the ugliness of the picture we are painting is unique in the sense that its scope and dangers have not been imagined before in the history of humankind. One danger is the threat of nuclear war and its potential for the self-destruction of Western civilization. Another is the threat of extinctions, including the biological species, ecological systems, and humankind, caused by climate change which, as we well know, is the result of our exploitation of the natural order for revving up our many machines. This puts America at the end, and perhaps the ending, of the course of Western Civilization, a place and position that has been seen as glorious in many ways, but now is sobering. We are not able fully to account for this new view of the world, but we can trace many of its features back into the history of the Western Tradition and acknowledge their current effectiveness in the way our society is working both for and against itself. All of these features can be traced to moments of invention and developments that became social interests. Some of these social interests have become industries, others have taken the form of research institutes; others are still being studied in depth by academic disciplines, such as the problem of individualism. Taken together as a set they are all products of persons who pursued questions of human interest about the way the worlds of nature and society worked. Each discovery became a matter of general acceptance by the people and can be called a *social interest*.

While working on the social theory of myth, I came up with the term *social interest* as a way to account for the link between some regular practice or feature of a tribe or nation that had been taken up into its mythic imagination and "painted" onto its big picture screen as a symbol of significance. The "interest" was "social" in the sense that it was shared by all the people, mostly as a self-evident feature of their lives together. In many cases the mythic symbol was a way to remember a primary activity such as the harvest of corn, or an important season such as the coming of spring. There were also myths surrounding the construction of a temple, or an irrigation system. In other myths it might be an important chief, warrior, or explorer who was remembered for an important discovery, ability, or period of the social history. Myths were the way in which what we now call *history* was recorded and remembered by tribal peoples. The historic reality of the mythic events did not seem ever to be questioned. This called for noticing what we might call the "gap" between the present and the past, on the one hand, and the difference between the social world of everyday and the memory of the mythic world, on the other. This social psychology of language and memory seems to work as a mechanism for all peoples and their cultures. It is important to underline this similarity of cultural anthropologies before going on. People live in two worlds at the same time. The mythic world makes it possible to understand the social world, and what other persons are up to who belong to the culture. It can be used to negotiate a relationship in shorthand in conversations because both parties will have shared the significance of the mythic datum referred to as a common symbol. The point is that the self-evidence of a mythic datum counts as a truism that cannot, need not, be analyzed critically in common popular discourse. It can also be taken up as an explanation for a circumstance that calls attention to itself, or as a symbol used for an artwork to evoke critical thinking about some feature or moment of social life.

It is also the case that, as a myth loses its immediacy and clarity of reference to the social order in the process of social change, its mythic features can continue in the popular imagination. They can continue as long as a mythic event or symbol is retained within a people's collective imagination and functions as still "memorable." That is because the mythic world, similar to that of a good novel, provides for a narrative context to see and understand a given moment or act. This orientation to another, bigger world and its narratives or systems of relationships and meanings does not immediately evaporate when a new set of inventions and projects appears and the structure of the society and its patterns of activity shifts or changes. It can continue as long as it has not been replaced by another set of mythic data to better account for and understand the changing social world in which the people live. This is the case with the Christian myth in America that continues to inform Protestant Christian attitudes toward others despite the many changes in our social history that do not agree with the original circumstances for the attitudes.

For now, it is important to see that new inventions and discoveries can easily become social interests in the course of a people finding them interesting and taking them up as important practices and projects for their society as a whole. Not having a place in an earlier mythic or social history, such social practices may become major social interests that do not have a symbolic significance according to the earlier mythic world. Thus the big picture can become a collector of the experiences and memories of many moments in which inventions and discoveries push the contours, size, and narrative links between the moments and events that give their projects placement and meaning. In the course of Western history, the emergence of several new social interests, such as Science as a pursuit and its effect upon the natural and material orders, has produced intellectual struggles to merge and coordinate the new social interests with the mythic world. Western cultural history is full of marvelous moments of human intellectual ability such as the accomplishments of Science, the methods of archeology,

Social Democracy

and the inventions of the printing press, the machine, the factory, and the market. Each of these moments has attracted artisans and others in the spread, development, and application of the invention to a wide range of practical and social pursuits. Some pursuits carry their primary description along as a designation, such as Science. Others receive new names, such as Capitalism. And others still are found to be important to the workings of a society and develop complex layers and networks of institutions, theories, and legislation, such as the worlds of Finance and Economy. Interests such as these can become subcultural worlds of their own and develop their own big pictures and mythologies. If we think of a social interest at the level of a social practice, its "mythology" may not need to be "painted" onto an erstwhile cosmic screen to compete with the older mythology that may still be there. But this can and has happened, as for example in the conflict between Science and Religion on the creation of the world. In other cases, the screen of a new myth may be an abstract concept, such as "man". In this case conflict can take place with other anthropologies in which a representative human figure is central (such as Adam), without needing to evoke them or search for arguments to solve the intellectual issues that arise between them. The point is that the social interests and practices of Western civilization have filled the collective memory screen with so many images of social significance that the older cosmic myth of Christendom cannot contain them. Insofar as myths are made in the course of human pursuits, and insofar as myths are the way humans paint the worlds in which they live, and insofar as the number of post-Reformation social interests and their myths are now at the point of cluttering the erstwhile (cosmic) myth of Christendom, Westerners no longer have a clear picture of a singular mythic narrative or symbol to provide for a common understanding of their social world with its social ethic and purpose for their society.

This consideration should help with the question of why there does not seem to be a common vision of a good society, and why the attempts to address conflicting opinions end up with yelling at one another instead of discussing alternatives to answer emerging issues. Discussions require common ground in a shared big picture in order to assess the significance of an issue and its consequences for the larger picture. Without that there will be no serious discussion. But this consideration does not yet explain the rancor and viciousness of the political attacks and "debates" that are occurring. How, for instance, does having a political position or program become so non-negotiable that its mention stops the conversation? What kinds of idea will not yield to further questioning? The answer is that the intellectual and political positions now being "discussed" are often anchored in different sets of myth fragments. Myths serve as a grammar for one's orientation and identity within a society. Myths of a religious or cosmic nature provide for the identity of a people as community and for an individual's orientation to its world. When a difference of opinion does not have a single collective vision in mind for the identities of the individuals, there may not be any meaning or purpose left to discuss. Identity is a very significant value in the social psychology of a people. It may be the fundamental value that bonds a person to its people and holds the people together as a community. In the current case of calling each other names in American politics and media, identity has become the basic issue at stake in all arguments, both for persons and for discourse. And that complicates the situation enormously. You cannot win an argument by offending the identity of one's opponent or assuming that the position of one's opponent is nonsense because it has to do with an identity that is different. As for the recent violence in Florida, mentioned in Chapter 4, note the words of Wayne LaPierre, the CEO of the NRA calling the protesters of the NRA *socialists* who want to restrict the individual's *right* "to bear arms," according to the U.S. Constitution, and all the *rights* of all persons. For him, these socialists want to take away all American *rights* to "freedom," and thus to change our society forever. It does not take much to see that the two sides of this issue have little in common about which to argue, much less discuss. Another illustration of such an impasse is the recent rant of Attorney General Sessions against mayor Schaaf of Oakland, California, who had warned city officials of plans by ICE to do a sweep of illegal immigrants in her city. Sessions said: "So here's my message to Mayor Schaaf: How dare you needlessly endanger the lives of law enforcement just to promote *your radical open-borders agenda?*" (*Los Angeles Times*, March 8, 2018, emphasis added.) There is no constructive response possible to such a personal attack. Their differences have to do with two entirely different worldviews. Schaaf would surely be able to spell out the progressive view of the State of California for discussion. But for Sessions to call her position a "radical open-borders agenda" tells us that his position is not only conservative, but is rigidly held as non-negotiable. He simply stopped the thinking required to engage the issue by shifting the issue from immigration to the violation of the law.

If we want to explore the possibility that the value of a term can be rooted in the mythic imagination of a speaker, we need to make one more observation about mythic mentality. It is that the grammar and syntax of a mythic mentality can continue to provide for one's identity even after the myth itself has begun to erode as the primary picture informing a society. Such is the case with the Christian myth. Its broad outlines and mythic grammar can still be at work in providing for the identity of Protestant Churches and individuals even after the society as a whole has focused on social issues and projects that are no longer anchored in the social logic of the myth. Many of the current ideologies that assume anchorage in the past can become a one word argument for a proposition that continues to be important as the name for an entire worldview in the mind of its users. Such is the rhetorical value and power of the Ku Klux Klan, White Male Supremacy, Nationalism, and No New Taxes. Other positions can try to tuck into one of the several charters used to justify a legality even when the charter is no longer working as a legal document, as in the case of the Southern appeal to the Bible to justify slavery, or even when the original meaning of the charter is violated, as in the appeal to the second amendment to support the right for individuals to bear arms. This means that, although our picture is now manifesting itself in ugly repartee, repainting cannot be easily imagined as a project of merely cleaning up our discourse. The issues are much more serious than the giving and taking of offense.

The serious issues have to do with the structure of our society, the way it works, and the consequences of its policies and actions. Many of us thought that our efforts aimed at becoming a federal union of states, and our brief history of amendments and agencies aimed at the revolutionary values of justice, equality, and freedom were surely on target to create a modern society of which we and the world could be proud. Instead our obsession with individualism and the freedoms from government control of industry, business, and finance available in the new world has resulted in a history of independent industries and private institutions that have created conflicts among the states ("nations") and their political orientations. On top of the basic differences caused by their various European extractions, and the uneven histories since the Second World War, the emergence of several social interests as major projects of the society have been institutionalized as competitors with one another and the government, thus creating overlaps and conflicts of interests that are now difficult for the government to control. The major projects have already been listed and partially discussed in earlier chapters and publications. They are the Military, Capitalism, Science, Finance, and Globalization. The "spreading of

Critical Times for America

Democracy" has been a term used to justify many of our activities abroad. But our involvement in the recent chapter of world history has not gone well, and we are now wondering what has gone wrong. We stumbled into fascism, used armies for protecting our "national interests," created agencies for the collection of secret intelligence, planned assassinations, oversaw massacres, allowed Capitalism to create an oligarchy of the wealthy, cultivated the fantasy of personal power and individualism, let nationalism be defined by racism, encouraged the sciences to create worlds of virtual reality for the populous, turned the concept of "mission" into one of global empire, let the Republicans off the hook with their single idea platform, allowed the Tea Party to take control of the Congress, let the president start dismantling the welfare state, let the Republicans tell the people they do not have the right to Federal monies, deported "foreign" immigrants, hardened our borders, and painted the future of a Great America that the rest of the world finds disgusting and dangerous. And we wonder why there is so much anger and violence among the people?

Neither Trump's picture of America's greatness, nor the continuing references to the Christian Nation can serve as the big picture we need to start working on the rectifications called for. If the crises we confront all have to do with the structure and operation of the society as a government, turned ugly by the self-serving interests of individuals mesmerized with wealth accumulation, and by politicians who easily disregard the welfare of the people, the root cause of our disease should be obvious. It can be diagnosed as the self-understanding of self-centered individuals who have not grown up, who have not left the adolescent stage of fighting on the sand lot rumble for juvenile glory. In such a case, the culture of the society at large is simply missing from one's experience and education. The larger social world of learning to appreciate the many skills and accomplishments of others in the production of culture was apparently avoided, or perhaps not there to be encountered. Human culture starts with social units like families who take their place as interested and knowledgeable participants in society. Society consists of larger networks of persons involved in personal and constructive projects, occasions for meetings with others for celebrations, displays of one another's skills and achievements, works of art, appreciations, discussions about events and problems that have occurred, local organizations of volunteers to provide aid for others who are not able to meet an unexpected emergency, and greatness in terms of personal performance and character. I remember the story of a barn raising after a fire that had burned it down.

Social Democracy

The people around pitched in, and the neighbor who knew how to get the job done and volunteered to supervise the building, was asked to lead the first dance in the new barn in his honor. The caller said "Good job, Joe." That was his pay, and his smile said it was more than enough. He was proud to be able to help his community out.

As for the picture of the Christian Nation that has been constantly called upon to imagine America's society, it can no longer be thought of in terms of the comprehensive cosmic myth of Christendom, nor in terms of the Protestant version of the myth based on the Bible and the Constitution. This myth of America's manifest destiny has run into trouble and no longer projects a positive future. The term is still being used among Christian congregations as some kind of claim on the past history of Christian kingdoms or perhaps on the Calvinistic concept of a Christian city important to early Yankeedom. But in application to the United States it has only become a shibboleth of the Republican party. The Bible can still be used to anchor an argument for a particular issue, but it can no longer justify atrocities. In the Deep South, for instance, slavery has been anchored in the Bible (Gen 9:18–27), lynching regarded as the just recompense of the wicked, and the American "missions" justified as honoring Jesus's command to "go and to make disciples of all nations" (Matt 28:18–20). With the social logics underlying this kind of *exegesis* (interpretation), and the actual practices that find the Christian Bible (myth) as justification, it is no wonder that the confessions of the Republican political candidates for the presidency and their discourse about the Christian Nation indicate an egregious failure of our national intelligence, not at all an honorable piety. This means that we simply do not have a big picture of a common good society to consult as we wonder about repainting the ugly pictue now before us.

At the end of my recent Yale book (*The Rise and Fall of the Christian Myth*) I made the suggestion that the social democracies in Europe were waiting in the wings to engage us in America about the kind of society we could be, supposing it dawned on us that a great deal about the ugliness in the world was a result of our own missions abroad. I was in Europe during the 1960s studying cultural history at the University of Göttingen. Bonnie, my spouse, was studying the English system of public education. We took time to investigate the post-war state of affairs in Germany, and visited several other European nations, both through Scandinavia to the North and to France, Spain, Greece, and Italy to the South. We learned that all of the European Nations still had the memories of the earlier French Revolution in mind, and especially the somewhat later fascist responses to the identity chaos of peoples and nations during the nineteenth and twentieth centuries. Nevertheless, each had found a way to restructure their older patterns of kingship, ward off authoritarian dictators, and call their peoples together in several attempts to agree on new sets of principles, laws, and congresses. All were working with some combination of democracy and Marxism, both as new concepts of governance in support of the well-being and welfare of the people this side of monarchy. The French set of democratic values was much in play, as well as the American Declaration of Independence. Several nations had already constructed wondrously balanced societies that they called *Social Democracies*. Bonnie and I were much impressed and could not help making constant comparisons between the European social democracies and what we knew as the democracy in America, sometimes called capitalistic democracy.

We lived in a small village near the East-West border where we could see the guard towers on the other side. We were taken in by the residents of this village, called Reckershausen, who invited us to their annual visit to the border where some still had families on the other side who, for this occasion, had come to the border and were standing on the other side of the doubly fenced barrier and waving to us. The people of Reckershausen helped us understand the folkways and attitudes of life "auf dem Land." They explained that the University of Göttingen known as an "Arbeitsuniversität" (where one went to work, not to play) gave Niedersaxony an honored place in German history and culture. It was a wonderful four years. No homeless people in Göttingen, Kassel, Cologne, Frankfurt, Berlin, Munich, or anywhere. No gun violence. No guns anywhere, in fact, except for those licensed to be used by the hunting clubs. They did not want or need them, they said, and kept asking us why every American needed one. There were many occasions for the local celebrations of life together, birthdays, the church choir party, the harvest festival parade, the trips to Göttingen for a political lecture. Close-by industries were humming. Buses and trains always on time. There were spirited discussions of cultural events among the teens at the restaurants in the villages and the students at the *mensa*s (tables at the university cafeterias). And everyone was aware of world news. When Kennedy was assassinated, we learned about it the same day from the local shopkeeper when we happened to be at his market. The local Baron invited us over for "wine evenings" so we could learn about the effects of the Thirty Years War on his ancestry, and on the local farms and villages. Everyone knew the ideological

Social Democracy

differences between the SPD (German Socialist Party) and the CDU (Christian Democratic Union). They thought it unfortunate that we did not have a social democratic party in America. There was opera in Kassel, forty minutes away. Theatre in Göttingen, fifteen minutes away. And there was jazz in the evening at the parties. An acquaintance of the Baroness had first heard jazz from the black American military personnel after the war. He said they gave the kids candy and taught them to play jazz if they could find an instrument at home in the attic. He explained that after the war American jazz became Germany's way of letting the black blues and syncopation heal some of the wounds of the war. All in all, we found the social democracies of Europe a strangely fitting response to the earlier fascisms that now counted as the first, but failed, attempts after the French Revolution to learn to live without a king. The American criticism of Sweden's social democracy often came to mind: "Their taxes are too high." We decided that Americans had just been hoodwinked by the Republican mantra. The Swedes had another picture of a social community and did not mind the taxes for which everyone had the benefit of health care and a society that worked well for all. In Germany it was a great relief for us to live in a society that did not have impoverished people without shoes on the streets.

America experienced the nineteenth and twentieth centuries without falling into fascism. We were preoccupied with the problems of forming a Federal Union of thirteen colonies. It was not a perfect Union, but it was a remarkable achievement, one of a kind as Woodard has reminded us. It was the creation of a democracy in which "freedom" was to be the controlling factor in the balancing of government, oligarchy, and the people for the pursuit of life, liberty and happiness. Never before in the history of humankind had a disparate people formed a society with such in view. That it happened in America instead of in Europe was due to the circumstance of a variety of peoples colonizing a new land, and the struggles of different colonies to negotiate different interests, each of them thinking about "government" on the model of their European experience. The struggles have not resided and the "more perfect union" has not yet appeared. But the brief history of the attempts to balance the three-way set of interests and forces that Woodard identified as the state, the financial oligarchy, and the people was enough to create a nation capable of making the decision to enter the Second World War and marshalling an industrial and military force of unsurpassing strength in a surprisingly short period of time. After the war America assumed the position of leadership among the nations that had been involved in the war, mainly by virtue of the fact that many had been devastated during the war and needed our help to restore their governments and economies. We were not conscious of the accidental circumstance (the Second World War) that launched us into this leadership role. The accidental aspect was the affect of our role in the "winning" of the Second World War only to find that the other nations needed our help to restore their countries from "losing" the war. A second surprise was the post war period of social welfare improvements (GI Bill and such) and economic growth (The Golden Age), which put us in the global spotlight and encouraged another amazing immigration of the "huddled masses yearning to breathe free." All we knew about dictators and fascism was what we saw happening on the other side of the seas.

Unfortunately, as we now know, a naiveté about our brief moment of wealth, supremacy, and military strength has produced an amazingly aggressive sense of superiority among some of our white males. Without realizing that our rise to world leadership was not planned, nor a result of any superiority in matters of political intelligence and global vision, these white males have moved into positions of Republican party leadership and now think to control both the nation and the world. The social democratic nations in Europe have also witnessed the emergence of white supremacy nationalists in resistance to the European Union and in response to an overflow of fugitives from the Near Eastern wars. But this feature of the European achievement in creating a union of social democracies cannot be used as an argument against the idea of a social democracy. The recent formation of a coalition between the SPD and the CDU in Germany, a first and truly great negotiation and political achievement, is a remarkable sign of the intelligence and energies still at work in the troubled Union. In American we do not have that kind of intelligence at work to think of a negotiated arrangement to solve our tricky times. The Republican lockdown on thinking has made it difficult to consider a social democracy. The political discourse has been moving in the direction of a white male supremacy and an "economic nationalism" for some time. The concepts we need to think with have all been consigned by the Republicans to their Democratic opponents, considered to be intellectual softies who are not strong enough to stand up for economic individualism, and who are castigated as disloyal Americans. As Vice President Cheney said to Joe the Plumber, in effect: "Don't vote for the Democrats. They want to take your money from you and give it to the poor, those who do not deserve it." So we need a discourse that

Social Democracy

can rehabilitate the terms and concepts required for thinking clearly about a social democracy as our best bet for the future.

The very term *social* has become tarnished in our public discourse. This lets us see just how far the concept of Communitarianism (Woodard's term) has atrophied in the American world oriented to Individualism. *Social democracy* cannot even be uttered, threatening the very term *democracy* that we stand for as a nation, and that we have represented around the world with our missions. *Socialist* all by itself is even worse, meaning that a person is a believer in *socialism*, a term that has been confused with communism in our discourse ever since Stalin, the cold war, and Senator Joseph McCarthy. That has been a most egregious rhetorical and intellectual violence in America, not called for at all as a way to think through the challenge of analyzing our own democratic principles and purposes in light of the post war situation. What makes it even worse, of course, is that in America we have an immigrant constituency that is *multicultural*. This sets us apart from most of the European nation-states who have found ways to build upon their nativist foundations without turning them into racist ideologies. They appear to have learned some lessons about the inadequacy of racial purity as a political principle from their fascist experiments and failures. We can, at least, hope so. In America we have not struggled with that issue until now, and its surfacing as "white male superiority" would be laughable if not so serious, given the many nationalities and cultures that have emigrated to America and now compose large percentages of our population. As a matter of fact, our mixed constituency turns out to be a major resource for the reconfiguration of our democracy that the times call for.

It is also the case that painting the picture of a social democracy for America would be the way to address, if not solve most of the social problems now threatening to tear our own union of states apart. A simple listing of these problems should be enough to ask the reader to consider a social democracy as the necessary next step for our own democracy to take. The present structure of the Unites States as a democracy does not need to be dismantled in order for a social democracy to emerge. The structure of the society is more than workable and it is working. The problems of these tricky times are rooted in the attitudes and interests of the political parties and politicians now in power. Woodard's emphasis on the *individualism* that has become a main feature of the American character is certainly correct. It is the only way in which the *freedom* we stand for has been interpreted and internalized in the social psyche. And the game board that makes it possible for the individual to compete, win, and display one's competence (if not superiority) is the money game made possible by capitalism. This remarkable game board has become the major feature of our patterns of activity and exchange, and its "values" are the way in which we immediately turn to discuss our projects. As George Skelton puts it in the *Los Angeles Times* (March 12, 2018), "Single-Payer care is a pipe dream." Why? It would cost too much! So the single plank platform of the Tea Party Republicans has won the capitalism game at the highest level of "thinking" and power in America. "We earned ours. Go earn your own." The naiveté that allows them to run for political office and promote their "Just say No" ideology is astounding. The reduction of social vision and perception to such a level is the root cause of most, if not all, of the major social issues and problems we have observed in this paper. We need only to mention the short list in order to say that a social democracy would be the answer.

There is the problem of aggression and anger, illustrated by the gun violence issue. I did not encounter any of this problem in Europe.

There is the health insurance issue. The Republicans cannot agree that every citizen has the "right" to health care. The term "right" is a legal concept used in our Declaration of Independence for the rights of all citizens to "Life, Liberty, and the Pursuit of Happiness."

There is the huge gap between the rich and the poor that violates the "balance" in our economic system, as Woodard, Chomsky, and others help us to see. The inability to close this gap is rooted in the political principles of the Southern Oligarchy Slave State that have frustrated every attempt to reform our systems of taxation and election.

There is the government's failure to control big oil, pharmacy, and Wall Street even though it is clear that they are taking advantage of the government for their own interests, leaving the consequences and costs for others to bear.

There is the current government's denial of climate change in the face of scientific projections of extreme danger. This is an outrageous impediment to rational thinking and democratic functions of a society devoted to intelligence and well-being.

There is the global mess we have made with our military, and the fact that our government continues to support the military as the answer to threats from other nations, many of whom now have weapons we have supplied. Thinking in terms of weapons to solve social problems is not only fallacious, it is delusional.

Social Democracy

This leaves us with a most curious situation. The history of Western civilization and culture has produced two exceptional arenas of nation states, the European and the American. Both have experienced successful economies and modern cultures. And both have struggled with the problem of creating a society without a monarch. In the case of Europe there was at first the horror of fascism and a few other missteps in the expansion of empires and their consequences for other peoples. But then the modern histories provided lessons that had to be learned about power, authority, diplomacy, negotiation, trade, and welfare. Most of the European nation states turned out to be brilliant students and produced marvelous welfare states. Then, with an eye on the bigger picture of multiple nations living together in Europe and on planet earth, they formed the European Union, withdrew their colonies, and organized conferences and congresses to tackle truly large scale global issues, such as climate control. These social democracies have not solved all of their problems, but as an achievement in the formation of a union of social democracies at the ending of Western history, they can certainly be congratulated.

The American story is now suffering a crisis of political configuration and social sanity. At first there would seem to be no solution to the impasse between the Republican and the Democratic parties now that Capitalism and Individualism have influenced their mentalities to such an extent. It is also the case that the election of Trump has revealed just how rigid and unmovable the mental effect of that influence can be, and how impossible it has been to have a conversation, much less a debate, with him and his Tea Party Republicans. This means that we have to add to our list of social issues matters of political inability and the way our politicians have abused the social structure. The two party system of political thinking seems to be unable to handle the basic functions of policy formation, much less execution, in their current lockdown of dissent. And the lack of reasonable discourse, much less rational debate on social issues and the purpose of government tells us that the many forms of protest among us have little chance of being heard. This crisis is much worse than the "critical times" I used to describe the problem. It is truly a social-psychological malady that, as Chomsky has said, is rushing us to the "cliff."

We need to relax and find a way to create another forum for thinking together about America and the state of the world. An article by Rana Dasgupta on "The Demise of the Nation State" (The Guardian, April 5, 2018) can help us see why both the nation-state and the state of the world have to be in the picture for serious discussion. He outlines the history of the nation-state to clarify the reasons for its creation, and the history of the recent globalization of financial, electronic, and democratic imperialisms to emphasize the fact that that larger picture of peoples, nations, and interests makes it impossible for a single nation to be in control of itself, much less the world. The energies and interests, as well as the political liaisons and arrangements that are now coming into being among nations throughout the world, should tell us that America is no longer in control, and that it cannot be in control of the new age which is to be identified as *global*. All of the marks of a nation-state's strength as a would be "leader" of nations are in the process of becoming obstacles in the context of globalization. The nation-state is no longer able to control its own corporations, for instance, or the flow of its own finances. It is now constantly dealing with "external forces" that impinge upon its internal arrangements and relations to other nations. These "forces" (Dasgupta's term) will not go away. And this means that Trump's slogan of "Greatness Again" is not only deceptive as a political ploy, it reveals an astonishing ignorance of the world he thinks to govern. What then about our nation-state? What then about the world? What then about a "social democracy"?

Dasgupta's vision (big picture) for the future of our societies cancels out the Trumps of this world, but it does not prophesy the likes of cliffs, exterminations, or nuclear war. He thinks the Western accomplishment of a social democracy is exactly what is right for the common good society of the future, and does not think its "demise" cancels it out. He paints the big picture of globalization as the new challenge facing Western civilization, and this is where the global vision gets very interesting. The "external forces" that impinge upon the single nation-state, and especially upon the one that wants to be the "leader" of nations, are all actually the "interests" (my term) of other nations that are caught up in the system of relations that globalization has created. These "interests" are those that should be understandable were we to back off and join the human race as one of the many. Dasgupta's vision is that of a "society of societies," a global form of adjudicating issues that arise among the many societies somewhat on the model of the European Union where the "constraints" against predation because of the union of the states can encourage cooperation in the interest of general well-being. The article is not really visionary in the sense of painting this picture as an ideal model for the future. It is a portrayal of the present conditions that pertain to the demise of the single state and the

Social Democracy

impossibility of continuing to think in terms of the outmoded interests in power, governance, and political control.

What if we thought it might be possible to have some of our intellectuals and political leaders find new ways to come together and discuss our situation not as a political issue, but as a social and national problem? The impression each of our leading politicians has given during the past two years of social concern is that they have to stay true to some sort of party ethic, taking care not to offend the protocols of their two party forums, and not to speak for any but themselves. Thus their speeches and papers are strictly occasional, addressing specific issues being talked about in the media and popular discourse, but seldom discussing issues in light of the overall state of the nation and explaining the reasons why their own proposals might matter. We the people have therefore not been instructed in the reasons for the appearance of an issue or the consequences of the many proposals and policies for addressing it in terms of the well-being of the society. If we could get a few social-democratic leaders and thinkers to consider such a proposition, we might ask them to think about becoming a "multiclass executive council" in charge of analyzing our social and political situation with respect to the roles we might better play in the current global context, and the policies required to better address the problems we are having with our society. A multiclass executive council could take the place of our current administration now in disarray and in need of overhaul. They could be "representatives" of our multicultural and multiclass society, using their new forum to be at work together instead of each seeking admittance to the oval office (which we might want to turn into an excellent venue for a cabaret). They would be busy discussing the histories and theories of social democracies, analyzing the current problematic social situations, writing papers with proposals for next steps, and regularly addressing the people on a live news medium (*non*-Fox News, of course; more like Roosevelt's fireside chats) to *explain* the social situations in relation to our histories, peoples, and values. They would also tell us their reasons for their proposals and what the consequences would be for our multicultural social democracy-in-the-making. Would not that be something to talk about, think about, and celebrate? If Elizabeth Warren's work on behalf of consumer protection could be explained to the people as part of a larger plan for the federal government's responsibility for the welfare of the people, and what all the welfare picture entails . . . If the significance of Chomsky's critique of capitalism could be spelled out as the major political issue of our time with some advice for the first steps to take for its control and reassignment . . . If Bernie Sander's clarity about the failure of government to reign in Wall Street could be turned into a full-fledged positive political platform for a social democracy . . . If Cornel West's reasons for thinking that "neoliberalism" was wrong could be explained to the people along with what the better form of liberalism should look like . . . If Jerry Brown's clarity about the issue of climate warming and what to do about it could become a national instead of a state project . . . If the leaders of the Women's March movement would say what they think needs to happen in Washington and throughout the country to guarantee the full range of equality they are talking about and how that would affect the entire range of political operations in our government and social life . . . If the youth leading the protests in Parkland could be asked to share their visions of a community without guns and what a national society then might look like . . . What a conversation and political event that would be! We would not need to hear any more from Trump, Bannon, Ryan, McConnell, Spencer, Bolton, or any of the Tea Party Republicans. We already know what they are thinking and that it is not only myopic, but absolutely dangerous. We might not need an electoral college or a two party system at all. We would, of course, have to figure out how to save the day for the present commissions and agencies of our once well working government without needing an autocratic Republican president. But would not that be exhilarating?

Give our multiclass executives a little time, and we may not have to pack for the trip to the cliff.

Conclusion
Repainting the Big Picture

This book was written in the turmoil of Trump's first year in office. His dismantling of the American society and tradition changed the plans for a sequel to my Yale book. The plan had been to describe a *Social Democracy* as the next best step for the United States, building on John McGowan's *Postmodernism and Its Critics* as well as a number of other studies about *Multiculturalism*. The Trump disaster effectively erased that plan, revealing the behavior and thinking of the Tea Party Republicans and the strange ideological narrowness of Trump, Bannon, Ryan, McConnell, Spencer, and many others that came to be called White Male Supremacy. I was not prepared for that, thinking that there was an underlying social sense of the values of freedom, equality, and justice that had long since been extended to the many cultural traditions among us, and that undergirded our two party democracy. Not so. The Trump disclosure was that the emergence of the Tea Party was rooted in deeply embedded prejudices that were just now surfacing, such as racism, male supremacy, military power fascinations, and the predatious motivations of our capitalistic economy. With the Republican lockdowns in the Senate, Congress, White House, and Supreme Court resisting any debate about social issues of concern for the people, there was little chance for a picture of a Multicultural Social Democracy to catch anyone's attention long enough even to be read and considered.

Critical Times for America

So Colin Woodard came to the rescue with his two-volume history of our *Eleven Nations*, and his explanation of the *American Character*. It clarified many of the reasons for the deeply embedded fixation on *Individualism*, and the failure of Republican political discourse even to consider the values of the *Communitarian* vision of a society that had the entire populous in mind. Woodard's study stayed at the level of historical description and the conflict of ideologies that determined the political decisions that occurred. I needed that, but noticed all along that this level of description and explanation did not reach deeply enough into the social psyche to engage my own interest in mythic mentality, or the startling manifestations of White Male Supremacy that were now surfacing. This meant that I had been mistaken all along when writing the last three or four books, thinking that an exposure of the social logic of the Christian myth would be enough to find a readership. Not so. And that meant that my plan to suggest a consideration of a multicultural social democracy also would not find an audience. What to do?

I had noticed the way in which the term *class* was being used in Republican circles to castigate the "new class" of liberal academics and their ideas as the class "to watch for" as the most important opponents of their *laissez-faire* policies. I had been cautious about the use of the term since its ominous association with Marxism and Communism where a "classless society" was one of the ways a post-revolutionary ideal was projected. Now this *faux pas* by a Republican set it free to be used for the consideration of a whole range of classes and classifications as the dictionaries said it was intended to be used. For the original plan for a book on a multicultural social democracy I had begun to collect some examples to paint a picture of the attractions and rewards of living with such a mixture of peoples. Los Angeles used to promote a celebration of our several cultures by having a musical event, sometimes at Olvera Street, sometimes in the park at the Symphony Hall. From the Mariachis to the New Orleans Jazz Ensemble and the St. Louis Blues, to the *No* operettas, the western guitar quartets, and the dance routines from many South American cultures, we were all there to soak up the atmosphere and find ourselves thinking how great it was to live in California. So it occurred to me that it might be possible at the end of this book to tease the reader's imagination by substituting "multiclass" for "multi-culture" (to get my own strokes into the picture), and a "multiclass council" instead of the President in his Oval Office (to imagine a Washington that did not need Trump any longer). This does slight both the social

Conclusion

democracy and the multi-culture that the original plan had in mind, both of which had been shot down by the Tea Party guns. But as Jonathan Z. Smith said on one occasion, in response to an opponent who chided him with a remark that what he (Jonathan) said was a joke, Jonathan said, "Sir, in my world there are times when a joke is the best argument I have."

Bibliography

Calvin, John. *Institutes of the Christian Religion*. 1536.
Chomsky, Noam. *Optimism over Despair: On Capitalism, Empire, and Social Change. Interviews by C. J. Polychroniou*. Chicago: Haymarket, 2017.
Coates, Ta-Nehisi. *We Were Eight Years in Power*. New York: One World, 2017.
Dasgupta, Rana. "The Demise of the Nation State." *The Guardian*, April 5, 2018.
James, Clive. *Cultural Amnesia*. New York: Norton, 2007.
Josephy, Alvin M., Jr. *The Nez Perce Indians and the Opening of the Northwest*. New Haven: Yale University Press, 1971.
Lorenz, Konrad. *On Aggression*. Translated by Marjorie Kerr Wilson. London: Methuen, 1966.
Mack, Burton L. *Christian Mentality: The Entanglements of Power, Violence, and Fear*. London: Equinox, 2011.
———. *The Christian Myth: Origins, Logic, and Legacy*. New York: Continuum, 2001.
———. *Myth and the Christian Nation: A Social Theory of Religion*. London: Equinox, 2008.
———. *The Rise and Fall of the Christian Myth: Restoring Our Democratic Ideals*. New Haven: Yale University Press, 2017.
———. *Who Wrote the New Testament? The Making of the Christian Myth*. San Francisco: HarperSanFrancisco, 1995.
McGowan, John. *Postmodernism and Its Critics*. Ithaca: Cornell University Press, 1991.
Mendenhall, Thomas C., et al. *The Quest for a Principle of Authority in Europe 1715–Present*. New York: Holt, Rinehart & Winston, 1948.
Mizruchi, Susan L. *The Science of Sacrifice: American Literature and Modern Social Theory*. Princeton: Princeton University Press, 1998.
Montagu, Ashley. *The Nature of Human Aggression*. New York: Oxford University Press, 1976.
Sharlet, Jeff. *The Family: The Secret Fundamentalism as the Heart of American Power*. New York: HarperCollins, 2008.

Bibliography

Weber, Max. *The Protestant Ethic and the Spirit of Capitalism*. Translated by Talcott Parsons. New York: Scribner, 1930 (German original, 1904–1905).

Woodard, Colin. *American Character: A History of the Epic Struggle Between Individual Liberty and the Common Good*. New York: Penguin, 2016.

———. *American Nations: A History of the Eleven Rival Regional Cultures of North America*. New York: Penguin, 2011.

www.ingramcontent.com/pod-product-compliance
Lightning Source LLC
Chambersburg PA
CBHW032235080426
42735CB00008B/863